Additional Books by Sam Hendricks

Fantasy Football Guidebook: Your Comprehensive Guide to Playing Fantasy Football

-Named one of Top 4 Fantasy Football books of All-Time by RotoNation.com
-Award-winning finalist in the Sports category of the National Best Books 2008 Awards, sponsored by USA Book News
-Finalist in the Sports category of the 2009 National Indie Excellence Awards

Fantasy Football Tips: 201 Ways to Win through Player Rankings, Cheat Sheets and Better Drafting

Released in the summer of 2009, *Fantasy Football Tips* has become an even bigger hit than *Fantasy Football Guidebook*, beating the one-year sales mark in only nine months of availability!

Fantasy Football Basics: The Ultimate "How-to" Guide for Beginners

Fantasy Football Almanac: The Essential Fantasy Football Reference Guide

The Almanac is unique in that Sam gives rankings based on different scoring systems and roster requirements. Scoring includes TD-only, performance and PPR formats. The Almanac also addresses auction values, IDP rankings and keeper/dynasty leagues.

Fantasy Football Almanac 2008
Fantasy Football Almanac 2009
Fantasy Football Almanac 2010

Financial Planning for Graduates (May 2011)

Just one more... (A fictional novel due in June 2012)

Media Coverage

Look for Sam's expert advice and rankings in Fantasy Baseball Index, Fantasy Football Index, Fantasy Football Pro Forecast and other fantasy sports magazines.

Sam also participates in a weekly "Ask the Expert" column at www.FantasyIndex.com

Also check out www.FantasyFootballGuidebook.blogspot.com or www.XPPress.com where Sam blogs throughout the year.

Fantasy Baseball for Beginners

The Ultimate "How to" Guide

By Sam Hendricks

Extra Point Press
Austin Texas
United States
www.XPPress.com
Library of Congress Control Number: 2010932285
ISBN: 978-0-9824286-9-6
Copyright © 2010 by Sam Hendricks
All rights reserved
Edited by Trish Hendricks

Visit the author at www.FFGuidebook.com
Visit the publisher at www.ExtraPointPress.com

Printed in the United States of America by Lightning Source

Bulk purchases, please contact info@ExtraPointPress.com

Version 1.1

Acknowledgements

A big hug and special thanks to my publicist, editor and communications specialist, Trish Hendricks. Without her support and assistance, none of my books would be as coherent as they have been these past few years. My mother, Fannie, also gets my biggest thanks since she always encouraged me to reach for new heights and always has a smile and love that cheers me up even to this day.

To my lovely wife Birgitte, I owe everything. She completes me. Her understanding of late nights watching baseball and football and even longer nights drafting in high stakes leagues thousands of miles (and seven time zones away) constantly amazes me. However, I fear our turf wars over the family computer have just started as she introduces the world to SewDanish, her Scandinavian Textile Art company that can be found at www.SewDanish.etsy.com and her blog at www.SewDanish.blogspot.com. Let the battle begin.

An appreciative nod to my friends and colleagues who put up with my fantasy ravings in the work place: Tom "Duck" Donalds, Richard "Sammy" Mills, John "Kuz" Kuczka. Ned "Neckless" Rudd, Charles "Tuna" Midthun, Tom "Hog" Behnke, Dean "Smurf" Reed and Mike "Spike" Hafermann!

Finally, to Addison Fauber, may you know a little more about Fantasy Baseball now.

Table of Contents

Chapter 1 Why Play Fantasy Baseball?

I started playing fantasy baseball in 1993 with a classmate named Chris in Phoenix, Arizona. Fantasy sports were not new to me at the time, since I was already a veteran of fantasy football. However, while football was a head-to-head, weekly contest for the masses, fantasy baseball was, and is, a daily fight against every fantasy team. Fantasy baseball is a statistic-driven, individual player-optimized six-month battle. Both fantasy sports have a lot going for them. I am going to tell you how to play fantasy baseball and also how to have fun doing it.

I have written this book as a simple, straightforward "guide" on how to play fantasy baseball. This book is a great gift for anyone who is just getting started or thinking about playing fantasy baseball. _Fantasy Baseball for Beginners_ is also great for anyone (parents, spouses, youngsters, etc.) interested in learning more about the game

In your hands is an easy, systematic guide for beginners on how to play fantasy baseball. I promise there will be no jumping around from front to back to middle. Just read this straight through to get the basics. There are no pictures, no cute diagrams and, hopefully, no condescending language. I do not want you to feel discouraged or stupid simply because you have questions about a hobby that millions of other people play.

The order of the book is designed to immerse you in fantasy baseball slowly and from the beginning. I am using the tried and true teaching method of "tell them what you want them to know and then give them a summary of what you told them." I am not going to repeat myself three times in each chapter. Important stuff is in bold and a summary is provided at the end of most chapters for those who like a little review.

We start with why you may want to play fantasy baseball and what is baseball and fantasy baseball; then cover their history and where to start. The next two chapters cover the rules (hint: there are no official rules but there are some standard ones that many leagues use) and scoring systems; both chapters are critical to playing well. Chapter 6 covers ranking players and is more of a reference for qualities and trends at these point scoring positions, but it is the perfect lead-in to Chapter 7 - Drafts, which provides draft preparation tips. But how do you know who to pick at the draft? Chapter 8 covers preparing for the draft, including many strategies and two I recommend (one easy and one hard). Once you have your players, what do you do with them? Chapter 9 discusses which players to start each week. The focus of chapters 10 and 11 is how to improve your team. Chapter 12 provides resources (books, magazines and websites). Chapter 13 covers auctions.

I follow the KISS (Keep It Simple Sam) principle-

Steps to playing FB
1) Pick/Join a league (Ch 3-5)
2) Prepare for the draft (Ch 6-8)
3) Make weekly roster decisions (Ch 9)
4) Improve your team (Ch 10 and 11)

I will use the male pronouns throughout this book, but it is written with no gender in mind. I do not mean to presume that all fantasy baseball players are male, but recent studies show that as many as 90% of today's players are men You will find no off-color jokes, no sexist remarks and no profanity here. Any person, male or female, young or old, can learn about fantasy baseball and not feel intimidated or chastised.

By the same token, I will use the abbreviation FB for fantasy baseball from now on. Paper is a valuable resource (think trees…OK, money). So, rather than waste space and money spelling out fantasy baseball each time I refer to it, I will simply write FB.

Finally, throughout this book I will use the term "owner" to mean you, the fantasy baseball player, since you are, in effect, the owner, manager and coach. If I say "player" it is in reference to a baseball player or athlete who plays or should eventually play Major League Baseball (MLB). I will use the term manager for MLB managers unless otherwise mentioned.

There are some common FB/MLB terms and acronyms, which you should familiarize yourself with in the box below:

C	=Catcher
1B	=First Base
2B	=Second Base
SS	=Short Stop
3B	=Third Base
MI	=Middle Infielder (2B or SS)
CI	=Corner Infielder (1B or 3B)
OF	=Outfielder
Util	=Utility Player
DH	=Designated Hitter
SP	=Starting Pitcher
RP	=Relief Pitcher
P	=Pitcher
HR	=Home Run
W	=Win
IP	=Innings Pitched/Played
ERA	=Earned Run Average
WHIP	=Walks and Hits per Innings Pitched
MLB	=Major League Baseball
K	=Strikeout
AL	=American League
NL	=National League
S	=Save

You will also see some common notations for player rankings and draft spots. Rankings are annotated after the position abbreviation so the 12th best 2B will be 2B12. The #1 SP on a team will be SP1. Draft spots are denoted by round and then the spot within the round after a decimal. So the first pick of the first round is 1.01. The 12th pick of the second round is 2.12. Therefore, we can have 1B15 drafted in the third round with the fifth pick (3.05)

I believe that 80% of FB production can come from 20% of the work. This is known as the 80/20 rule of FB. The key is knowing what 20% to do and…deciding if the other 20% performance from 80% more work is worth it. I intend to show you that with my easy and hard draft strategies. The easy way is just that…easy. Will it win you a championship? It may or it may not. The hard way takes more effort and work but generally results in better production. (If that extra effort is worth it to you –you be the judge).

Woody Allen is quoted as saying, "80 percent of success is just showing up." The same thing can be said for FB. If you attend the draft (versus getting someone else to draft for you), you will have a better team. Putting in a few minutes of effort each day before the first game and setting your lineup day in and day out will prevent many FB mistakes in roster management. Reading the notes provided by your league website about your fantasy players can stop a season-ending error. All of these things are easy and not too time consuming. They are the FB equivalent of "just showing up." Do these things and 80% success is yours.

I was lucky enough to fly RF-4 and F-15E fighter jets in my Air Force career. Fighter pilots do not have time to debate all of the possibilities when flying at 600 miles an hour or at 300 feet off the ground. They need hard and fast rules to follow and a method for quickly determining the right choice. Fighter pilots use checklists and that is what I am about to provide you. You will find checklists for how to pick a league, how to rank players, and how to decide who to start. Checklists provide you with 80% success for only 20% of the work.

I have several books out, the most recent is _Fantasy Football Basics: The Ultimate "How-to" Guide for Beginners._ If you are contemplating fantasy football, this book is for you. You may wish to purchase one of my other books too, which are for more intermediate or advanced fantasy football players. My first book, _Fantasy Football Guidebook: Your Comprehensive Guide to Playing Fantasy Football,_ has done quite well (a second edition came out in March 2010) and is often referred to as the "encyclopedia of fantasy football." It is 400+ pages of information and is for the more advanced fantasy football player. It is all-inclusive, but many times people ask for just my personal tips on fantasy football. That is why I published _Fantasy Football Tips: 201 Ways to Win through Player_

Rankings, Cheat Sheets and Better Drafting. *Fantasy Football Tips* is for the fantasy football player who wants to know the best tips. It really is the best of the best.

Fantasy football is extremely popular for several reasons. One is the weekly head-to-head competition it encourages. This weekly battle between fantasy teams is easy to manage since an hour before the first kickoff owners can brush up on news and injuries and set their lineup. FF is also determined on one day either Sunday or Monday night.

But I digress.

Back to baseball. Whether you are a newbie who wants to learn what everyone (and I mean everyone) is talking about or a casual player who wants to know more about the game, this book is for you. Options, options, options, there are so many. I will get you through it.

Anyone will be able to find exceptions to this book and pick things apart with "my league does this" and "my league does that." Just remember: The answer to many questions is "it depends." It usually depends on your scoring system or rules, or both. Sometimes it will depend on your willingness to take a risk.

And no matter why you start (whether it be a local work league or a way to stay in touch with old friends or reconnect with a child), once you start, I guarantee you will be hooked. Don't say I didn't warn you!

Fantasy Baseball for Beginners is meant to be clean, simple and functional. No cute cartoons or complicated charts or diagrams - just easy to implement ideas, checklists and rules to follow. You be the judge if I succeeded. Good luck and, as always, drop me a line or a question at info@FFGuidebook.com or contact me through my publisher at info@ExtraPointPress.com

Chapter 2 What is Baseball and Fantasy Baseball?

MLB (Major League Baseball)

Before anyone can begin to learn about fantasy baseball, they need to have a basic understanding of major league baseball. If you already have a good grasp of baseball, skip ahead to "what is fantasy baseball."

According to Wikipedia:

"Baseball is a bat-and-ball sport played between two teams of nine players each. The goal is to score runs by hitting a thrown ball with a bat and touching a series of four bases arranged at the corners of a ninety-foot square, or diamond. Players on one team (the batting team) take turns hitting against the pitcher of the other team (the fielding team), which tries to stop them from scoring runs by getting hitters out in any of several ways. A player on the batting team can stop at any of the bases and later advance via a teammate's hit or other means. The teams switch between batting and fielding whenever the fielding team records three outs. One turn at bat for each team constitutes an inning; nine innings make up a professional game. The team with the most runs at the end of the game wins.

The game is played on a field whose primary boundaries, the foul lines, extend forward from home plate at 45-degree angles. The 90-degree area within the foul lines is referred to as fair territory; the 270-degree area outside them is foul territory. The part of the field enclosed by the bases and several yards beyond them is the infield; the area farther beyond the infield is the outfield. In the middle of the infield is a raised pitcher's mound, with a rectangular rubber plate (the rubber) at its center. The outer boundary of the outfield is typically demarcated by a raised fence, which may be of any material and height (many amateur games are played on fields without a fence). Fair territory between home plate and the outfield boundary is baseball's field of play, though significant events can take place in foul territory, as well."

A picture is worth a thousand words. So here is a typical baseball field.

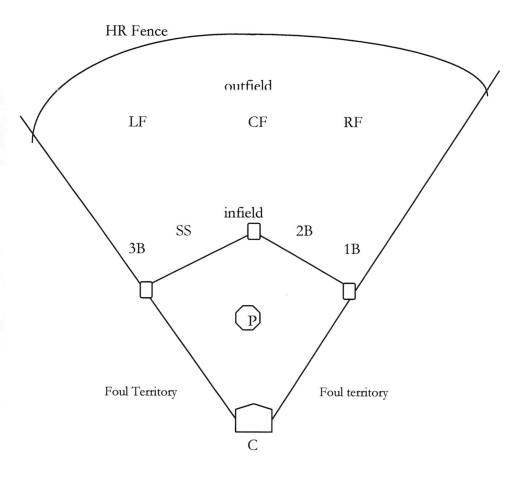

Baseball is America's pastime. But what is baseball; how do you play it?

At the beginning of each half-inning, the nine players on the fielding team (team not batting) arrange themselves around the field. All of the fielding players wear gloves to catch the hard ball (baseball) once it is hit by the wooden bat by the batter (opposing team's player).

The pitcher (P) stands on the pitcher's mound (exactly 60 feet 6 inches away) and throws the baseball towards home plate (which the batter defends). Should the batter not swing at or miss the pitched baseball, then another player, the catcher (C), squatting behind home plate, attempts to catch the baseball and return it to the pitcher. The remainder of the fielding team faces the batter. Generally, there are four infielders, three of whom line up near the three bases (1B, 2B and 3B). The other infielder, called a short stop (SS) plays between 2B and 3B, since most hitters are right-handed and will hit/pull the ball to their left. The outfield has three players: the right fielder (RF), the left fielder (LF) and one in the center called the center fielder (CF). Additionally, four umpires are on the playing field to make rulings.

The game starts with a batter waiting for the pitcher to pitch the baseball. If a batter hits the ball into the field of play (not into foul territory) he drops the bat and runs toward first base. If he can reach first base before the other team touches first base in possesion of the ball, then he is safe (called a hit). Reaching 1B on a hit is a single. Otherwise, he is out. He is also out if the fielding team catches the hit ball before it touches the ground. The batter can attempt to go beyond first base on his hit. If he reaches second base, it is called a double. If he reaches third base, it is called a triple and if he gets to home plate or hits the ball over the outfield fence within the foul lines, it is a home run (HR). A HR is the best possible outcome for a batting appearance. If the batter reaches base because of an error by the opposing team, then he does not get a hit on his batting statistics—instead, the fielder is charged with an error.

Players on the bases after batting are called base runners. Base runners can advance by batted balls that are not caught by the fielders or even if balls are caught (flied out) if they wait on base until after it is caught (called tagging up) they can then attempt to advance. Another way for a runner to advance is to try to get to the next base while the pitcher is throwing to home plate. This maneuver is called stealing and, if sucessful, results in a stolen base (SB).

Batters who hit the ball but are out because it is caught before touching the ground are said to have flied out. A ground out occurs when the batter does not reach 1B before the ball gets to first base.

Pitches not hit by the batter into the field of play are either a strike or a ball. If the batter swings at a pitch and misses it is a strike. If the batter does not swing, then it is based on the umpire's opinion of whether or not the pitch passed through the strike zone. The strike zone is the area over home plate from the batter's knee up to the midpoint between his shoulders and belt. If a pitch is in the strikezone the umpire calls it a strike, otherwise it is a ball. Note even if the pitch is outside the strike zone, if a batter swings and misses it is a strike. Once a batter accumulates three strikes, he is out. In this case, the pitcher is awarded a strikeout (K). A batter against whom four balls are recorded is awarded a base on balls (BB) or a free "walk" to first base. In the rare instances when a batter is hit by the pitch, he gets a free advance to first base. A ball hit but not in the field of play (in foul territory-a foul ball) is a strike as well, except it can never be the third strike to cause a batter to be out. In this case, with two strikes already against him a batter can foul as many pitches as possible. One exception to this rule is if the batter is attempting to bunt, then a foul with two strikes is his third strike and he is out. If the foul ball is caught, the batter is out.

The five most common ways for the fielding team to record an out are:

- The **strikeout**: against a batter who makes three strikes before putting the ball into play or being awarded a free advance to first base.

- The **flyout**: against a batter who hits a ball in the air that is caught by a fielder, whether in fair territory or foul territory, before it lands.
- The **ground out**: against a batter who hits a ball that lands in fair territory which, before he can reach first base, is retrieved by a fielder who touches first base while holding the ball, or relays it to another fielder who touches first base while holding the ball.
- The **force out**: against a runner who is required to attempt to advance—either because the runner is on first base and a batted ball lands in fair territory, or because the runner immediately behind on the basepath is thus required to attempt to advance—but fails to reach the next base before a fielder touches the base while holding the ball.
- The **tag out**: recorded against a runner who is touched by a fielder with the ball or a glove holding the ball, while the runner is not touching a base.

A player's turn at batting (at bat) can result in either a hit, out or advance to first base via walk or hit pitch. If the third out of the inning occurs because a base runner is caught attempting to steal a base (CS), then the batter gets another plate appearance in the next inning since he did not get his full at bat. Once a player's turn at batting occurs, he will not bat again until the other eight team members take their turn. In other words, the order in which a team bats (batting order) stays the same throughout the game unless a player is replaced by a substitute.

The american league has a designated hitter (DH) rule that allows the DH to take the place of another player (almost always the pitcher) in the batting order. However, the DH does not take the field. So, the american league has a team of 10 starting players; nine fielders and a DH.

MLB teams have 25 players on their rosters. Normally, this will be their eight starting fielders, five starting pitchers (SP), six relief pitchers (RP) and then six backup players. Many teams will have one or more backup catchers, two infielders, two outfielders and a specialist at hitting (pinch hitter; DH) or another pitcher.

There are 30 MLB teams divided into the National League (NL) and American League (AL). Each league has three divisions: East, West, and Central. However, there are 14 teams in the AL and 16 teams in the NL. The major league champion is determined by playoffs that culminate in the World Series. Four teams make the playoffs from each league: the three regular season division winners, plus one wild card team.

American football, soccer, basketball and hockey all involve a team effort playing on the same sized playing area for a set amount of time that requires a game clock. Baseball is unique in that it does not involve a clock, nor is it played in exactly the same sized venue and is more about a man to man struggle then a collective team effort. Anyone who has visited Boston's Fenway Park and Colorado's Coors Field know that the nuances of each field can affect the outcome. Just as anyone watching Steven Strasburg (WAS, SP) pitch knows that his ability determines the score more than most other team factors. I say baseball is America's pastime for good reason.

So now you know a little about MLB. But what is FB?

What is Fantasy Baseball?

You may have heard your co-workers talking about it in the office last year or your son is interested in playing this year with his school friends. In any case, you need to know what is so magical about this thing called FB. Everyone seems to be involved with it, but you just do not get it.

More than 30 million people play fantasy sports, so something must be special about it. You may have heard vague references to a "draft" and "players" on a team and not starting the right player. Don't fret, all will be revealed.

Basically it is a game of "I am better than you are" at MLB knowledge. I know more about who is going to do well statistically than you... But how does one decide who is the better baseball aficionado or expert? You and I might decide to pick players from each position (C, 1B, 2B, SS, 3B, OF, SP and RP) and then see which "team" does the best over the season.

How do we measure success? By who has the most HRs or most saves, in the case of relief pitchers?

In that case, you may rightly point out a foul if one or more of your players becomes suspended and is out for the season. "That's not fair!" you cry; "I should at least get a chance to replace my suspended players just as they do in MLB". Therefore, we change our little contest and allow FB "owners" to drop players and add new ones. The next point of contention is if some of my SPs are dinged up for a few weeks and thus drag my Wins and Ks down, because they are not pitching when they are injured. In this case, we modify the rules and only start a limited number from each position, so that "owners" can decide which players they expect to perform the best. In fact, we decide to make it just like MLB, where 1 C, 1B, 2B, SS, and 3B start and 3 OFs and 5 SPs and 1 RP start each week.

Now take our two-owner contest and expand it to eight to twelve other co-workers, friends or relatives who think they know more than we do and you have a league. Before the season starts, the league has a draft to determine which owner gets which players. This is usually a lively afternoon of fun where owners get to look each other in the eye and puff up their chests about how smart they are. Owners take turns picking players, who are then exclusively on just their team, (i.e. C.C Sabathia (P, NYY) can only be on one team in the league). The rules determine how many total players are on each team, how many players from each position must start each week, and how each player scores.

There is a great sense of pride in putting together your "hand-picked" team and coaching them to a championship; especially when it means beating your friends and neighbors. In fantasy baseball, you are the owner, general manager (GM) and coach of a team of MLB players. Complete with all the decisions that go with it, but without the millions of dollars it would cost.

Here is how it works. First you name your team. Even in names the New York Yankees are first since "Evil Empire" is one of the more common names. Then in a draft, just like in MLB, you get to pick players to fill your roster. Each week (or day?) you will decide who to start and who to bench. As the owners, you can make trades with other teams (if they agree) or drop players who are not performing and pick up others from a free agent pool (players not drafted in the draft or dropped by another owner). Your objective is to have the best regular season record (by winning each week), advance to the fantasy baseball playoffs and, eventually, win the FB World Series or score the most fantasy points. Throughout it all, the experience is a major ego trip since you drafted them, you own them and you determined who would play or start for the week.

How much time will it take? Fantasy baseball is a pursuit that takes as little or as much time as you want to give it. I have friends that I have introduced to the game who become very engaged (read obsessed) and devote many hours trying to get an edge. I have other friends that spend an hour or so before the games begin for the week and use that time to set a lineup. The most fun comes in the bragging rights of knowing you met your opponent in a head-to-head match up and came out with a victory. Remember, the winner of the fantasy baseball championship will have a year's worth of bragging rights.

What is the attraction of fantasy baseball? I am asked this all the time! So I came up with the Top 8 reasons to play FB. Hopefully, you can find one for you.

Top 8 Reasons to Play Fantasy Baseball

1) You love to watch baseball and your favorite team is driving you crazy.

2) Competition with other baseball fans. Players enjoy the opportunity to match their skills against co-workers, friends, and family members. One survey reports that 3 out of 4 fantasy sports participants play with others they know personally. Most men are competitive and this allows us to compete without getting off the couch.

3) Fantasy baseball gives you one more reason to cry, laugh, yell, scream, rant or jump for joy while watching Major League Baseball. It is like gambling but without the guilt.

4) The social aspect of belonging to a group appeals to some; not to mention social networking or sharing a hobby with your children or spouse.

5) Fantasy baseball helps you appreciate all of the talent in MLB, not just the talent on your favorite team.

6) Fantasy baseball makes for better MLB fans. We are more educated about the nuances. We are more aware of the player's skill sets. We care about the rules and the changes each year brings. We are more attuned to MLB.

7) Sometimes you watch a game to see how one or more of your players will do. Other times it is to see how your opponent's player does. Still other times it is to see how a player you are considering adding to your team is doing. Bottom line, you watch more and different games.

8). You want to win, have fun and have something to brag about around the water cooler at work (or at family gatherings). It is for the adrenaline rush of winning.

What are the Arguments Against Fantasy Baseball?

1) Fantasy baseball is gambling. Oh my! If a hobby that asks for an entry fee (to pay for the costs of running the thing) and gives a few baubles (bucks) back (and maybe a trophy) to the winner is gambling, then so is golf, bowling, bridge, and so on. Gambling should be where everyone has an equal chance of winning. Fantasy baseball is not a place where everyone has an equal chance of winning. You win by preparation, some luck, skillful drafting and season transactions. Gamblers play against the house. Fantasy baseball players play against their friends. In fact, Congress declared FB was not gambling with their 2006 legislation (see History of FB later in this chapter).

2) It takes up too much time. Actually, it will only take as much time as you want to put into it. If the family wants to go to Wally World this weekend, take them. Just make sure you set a lineup before you leave. Don't worry, I will provide you with easy steps to minimize the time spent.

So I ask again, what is fantasy baseball? It is a way to enjoy the game of baseball on a higher level. It is a method of competing while watching the sport you love. It is also a hugely popular social event. Anyone who has ever attended a draft knows the camaraderie and excitement of this one day of the year. It will be something to look forward to year after year. It is Christmas in March. It is about using your brain to best your friends in a challenging, yet non-threatening way. It is about getting together, laughing at other's picks, sharing outrage as your pick is snatched from you and looking forward to the upcoming season with optimism. It is the ultimate extension of the baseball season.

History of Fantasy Baseball

Daniel Okrent is credited in most circles as the inventor of modern rotisserie baseball in 1980. The name rotisserie comes from the name of the restaurant (La Rotisserie Francaise) where the league met and played. They also met at P.J. Moriarity's but that name did not quite fit. The first rotisserie league (called the Rotisserie League) had 10 owners (many were Philadelphia Philly fans) and was a NL only league (meaning they only used players who were in the National League). Another little known fact is that it was an auction league ($260 budget). Mike Schmidt was the first player auctioned on April 13, 1980 and went for $26 according to ESPN. Each team had a roster of 23 players. Watch "Silly Little Game" a movie that is part of ESPN's "30 for 30" series for more history.

Since Mr. Okrent (team name Okrent Fenokees) was a magazine writer/editor, many of the owners in his new league were journalists. Thus the "new" hobby received media attention almost immediately. The 1981 MLB strike proved to be a catalyst as many sports writers found themselves without their usual hunting ground (baseball play) for stories.

In March 1981, Dan Okrent wrote "The Year George Foster Wasn't Worth $36." In this _Inside Sports_ magazine essay, he publishes the rules of his rotisserie league. Bantam Books pulbished Okrent and the league's book _Rotisserie League Baseball: The Greatest Game for Baseball Fans Since Baseball_ ($5.95) in 1984.

The idea of picking players and running a baseball contest based on their statistics had been around a long time before 1980 and Daniel Okrent. Alan Schwarz, in his book _The Numbers Game_, tells of Harvard sociologist William Gamson and his "Baseball Seminar." Colleagues competed with rosters based on a player's

RBI, ERA and wins. One of these colleagues was University of Michigan professor Bob Sklar (an owner in Okrent's Rotisserie League), who taught it to Daniel Okrent. The rest is, as they say, history.

I would be remiss if I did not write of the Greater Oakland Professional Pigskin Prognosticators League (GOPPPL). As mentioned in _Fantasy Football Basics: The Ultimate "How-to" Guide for Beginners,_ GOPPPL is the start of fantasy football in 1962. But Bill Winkenbach had the same idea for fantasy baseball and golf around that time. Could he be the founder of both fantasy football and baseball? What of Glassboro State College, which formed a similar baseball league in 1976, four years before Okrent's.

No history of fantasy baseball would be complete without acknowldeging Bill James, the father of Sabermetrics, and his 1977 self-published book _The Bill James Baseball Abstract_. Although not for fantasy baseball specifically, it has advanced the game in many ways.

Another book that helped build fantasy baseball's momentum was _Baseball SuperSTATS_ by Ron Shandler in 1986. Fantasy sports products began to pop up. One of which was Fantasy Sports magazine in 1987, as the first multi-sport publication. Fantasy Baseball Index magazine started in 1994 with Barry Bonds as the #1 overall player.

The computer made calculations easier. As software became available, interest increased. The 1990s brought more FB information. USA Today started a weekly column on FB by John Hunt in 1993. Hunt started one of the first Expert FB leagues with the League of Alternative Baseball Reality (LABR). Prominent owners included Peter Gammons, Bill James and Keith Olbermann.

The internet (thank you, Al Gore) proved to be the big catalyst that propelled FB into fame. Stats could now be quickly calculated online without the tedious math (work) requiring paper, pencil and calculator. The internet took FB from sports bars and office lounges into individual homes and turned the hobby into a money-making enterprise. In 1999, Yahoo offered fantasy sports for free and an explosion occurred.

Next came high-speed internet, live scoring and real time stats, so that an owner could instantly see how his team was doing against his opponent. This burst in technology opened the door to high stakes, high profile, nationwide tournaments. The first multi-city, high stakes FB event occurred in 2004 when the National Fantasy Baseball Championship (www.NFBC.fanball.com) opened in Las Vegas, New York and Chicago. The NFBC drew 195 teams at $1,250 each for the main event and awarded the first $100,000 grand prize for FB. NFBC has since expanded to five cities and in 2009 had 390 owners participating in the main event.

In the history of FB several key legal issues occurred. I will not go into too much detail on either but both represented a danger to FB.

CDM vs. MLB involved the use of MLB player names/statistics and licensing deals with certain fantasy sports companies. MLB attempted to prevent companies from using player names and statistics without paying a license fee (not all companies were offered the license, thus others asserted the MLB wanted a monopoly over the industry). It was a defining moment in fantasy sports history when the judge ruled that statistics are part of the public domain.

In October 2006, President George W. Bush signed into law the Unlawful Internet Gaming Enforcement Act of 2006. The bill makes transactions from banks to online gambling sites illegal. What is significant is the law exempts fantasy sports games, thus defacto proving fantasy sports is not considered gambling.

By 2008, 30 million people in the United States and Canada were playing fantasy sports, spending $800 million on the hobby. Another high stakes competition returned in 2010. The World Championship of Fantasy Baseball (www.WCOFS.com) began again. Today, fantasy baseball is big business.

Fantasy baseball has progressed from small local leagues that used paper, pencil and the box scores to automated websites that give you live scoring. What started as ten people getting together in a restaurant in 1980 has become an international phenomenon with players and leagues across the globe.

Timeline for Fantasy Baseball History

1960 – Baseball seminar started at Harvard by William Gamson

-----------------------1970-1979--

1976 – Glassboro State College league formed

1977 – The Bill James Baseball Abstract self-published by Bill James, the father of Sabermetrics

-----------------------1980-1989--

1980 – Fantasy Baseball rules born in NYC restaurant La Rotisserie

1984 – Rotisserie League Baseball by Daniel Okrent published

1986 – Baseball SuperSTATS book published by Ron Shandler

1987 – "Fantasy Baseball" Magazine first published

-----------------------1990-1999--

1990 – The World Wide Web debuts as a new interface for the internet

1994 – "Fantasy Baseball Index" Magazine first published

1994 – League of Alternative Baseball Reality (LABR) formed (first Experts league)

1997 – Tout Wars league formed to rival LABR.

1999 – Yahoo adds fantasy sports for free

1990-1999 Rapid growth due to the internet

-----------------------2000-2009--

2004 – National Fantasy Baseball Championship (NFBC) begins

2006 – CDM vs. MLB, judge rules that statistics are public domain

2006 – The Anti-gambling bill has fantasy sports carve out language. It says that fantasy games are exempt from the gambling law as long as they meet two requirements:

1) Awards and prizes must be stated prior to game starting and not be determined by number of participants or total entry fee revenue

2) Winning outcomes are determined by skill for contests that use results from multiple real life games

In essence, it solidifies the fact that fantasy sports are games of skill, not luck

-----------------------2010--

2010 - Fantasy Baseball for Beginners published

2010 – The World Championship of Fantasy Baseball (WCOFB) begins again

Chapter 3 Where do I start?

You may not have a choice. If you have been invited to play with friends, relatives or co-workers, then you have no say in what type of league you join, since it is already formed and waiting for you to jump in. If you said yes, then the best you can do is learn from this chapter about how to play in your new FB league. For other readers, you may not be committed to any league yet. If this is the case, read on carefully and decide which type of league you will enjoy the most. My recommendations are highlighted in bold type and repeated in the chapter summary.

When I say "Avoid," it means to try not to play in such a league or follow that strategy. Notice I do not say "Never." I know it is hard to find the perfect league. I have been trying for 17 years now. In some cases, you will not have any choice in the league rules (if you were asked to join a local league). If so, just keep these thoughts in mind when it comes time to propose rule changes or if deciding on another league.

Free or Pay

Your first choice is this - Do you want to spend any of your hard-earned cash playing FB? Some leagues are free to play. Some charge a small administrative fee to pay for league expenses like the website, draft board, trophy and management firm that calculates the league statistics. Other leagues charge an entry fee so that they can award prizes (like a coffee mug, cash or even a ring).

If this is your first year in FB, I suggest keeping it simple and playing only in a free league or small administrative fee league. If you play in a pay league, make sure the fee is appropriate for the services provided. $15 should be more than enough to cover administrative costs. I do not recommend playing in a cash prize league when you are just starting out. Once you have a few years under your belt and feel more confident, then you can start putting your money where your mouth is. There is one large problem with free leagues - apathy. In many of these leagues the owners who are not in contention will quit on their teams. So you get what you pay for. Leagues where some prizes are involved tend to have more owner involvement. Free leagues …well, owners lose interest if they are not in the running to win late in the season. This is very frustrating, especially to a beginner who wants to play competitively. You were warned.

Here are some sites where you can join a free FB league ranked in order of my preference:

1) ESPN (http://ESPN.com)

ESPN has some of the best draft preparation tools around. The graphics are cool and crisp. Simply placing a cursor over the player gives the latest information on him. They also added auction capability in 2010. They are the best free service and have the most customizable leagues. The owners are somewhere between Yahoo's casual fans and the more diehard CBSSportsline owners. My only criticism is the silly ESPN jingle that plays every time you are up to draft.

2) Yahoo (http://yahoo.com)

YAHOO went free in 2010. They are the simplest and perhaps easiest to play in. But this can be both good and bad. Simplicity often breeds complacency. You will find many newbies like yourself and also some not so dedicated fans as well. YAHOO sees some of the highest no shows and autodrafting rates. They are generally recognized as the most played of these three free sites. One final point in YAHOO's favor is the tie in with their mail and website functions.

Although easy to use, I do have one complaint with the YAHOO draft room. The player drafted by others does not give position. This is tough on beginners since you spend quite some time looking for players to cross off your cheat sheets. The chat function actually does mention the position of the player drafted but that takes some getting used to.

3) CBSSportsline (http://CBSSportsline.com)

They have free leagues and a commissioner service for $179 per league. Since they have such a reputation as a commissioner service there are more dedicated teams playing here. Owners tend to pay more attention to their teams and thus there is less "dead wood" on their site.

Cash prize leagues or "money leagues" can be found in many of the same places as the free leagues, but they are run as private leagues (see below). You play by paying the entry fee. Be wary of these leagues if you do not know the commissioner (the person running the league).

There are low stakes money leagues, medium stakes leagues and high stakes leagues. I categorize the low money leagues as less than $100 for the entry fee. Medium stakes leagues are $100-$999 entry fees and high stakes leagues cost at least $1,000 to play ($1,300 for NFBC; $1,650 for WCOFB).

Each of the high stakes leagues have satellite leagues where you can play for around $125. I prefer to play in well-established leagues run by professionals such as the small satellite leagues from:

1) National Fantasy Baseball Championship (NFBC) (www.nationalfantasychampionship.com)

2) World Championship of Fantasy Baseball (WCOFB) (http://wcofs.com/site/wcofb).

Public or Private

Your next choice is public or private. Public leagues are available to everyone and can be found at major websites such as the ones mentioned previously. **I recommend a public league unless you have been invited to join a private league where you know some of the players or the commissioner.**

Entry into private leagues can only be through the approval of the commissioner (the owner running the league). This may be an invite-only league where only co-workers, friends or relatives are invited or it may be only for certain types of players (for example women only, New York Mets fans or those wishing to play for cash prizes).

Along the same lines as choosing a public or private league, there is a choice between playing in a local or a national league. A local league is one run by someone you know that involves people bound together by some bond (work, school, neighborhood, relatives). Whereas a national contest like the NFBC, WCOFB or their satellites involve owners from all lifestyles and all over the world simply playing to win money and be the best.

Rotisserie, Head to Head (H2H) or Points Based

Now that you have decided on some of the other variables, you need to decide on the format for competing. **Rotisserie** (also called Roto) is the most common way to play FB. In this type of league, teams are ranked from first to last in each statistical category. Points are awarded based on the number of teams in the league. In a 12-team league, the maximum points (total number of teams, thus 12) are awarded to the first place team in each category. The team with the second best statistics receive 11 points and so on until the worst team in each category receives 1 point. In a 10 category league, the maximum points any team can score (12-teams) is 120 points. The least possible score is 10 points. Overall ranking is determined by the total points scored from all categories.

H2H is where each owner plays another owner each scoring period (normally a week) and the team with the most fantasy points that period gets a win. H2H can be more exciting as it is always fun to beat someone else. However, the schedule (who you play and when) can affect outcomes. Rotisserie leagues tend to be fairer, but offer less excitement. Therefore, it is a trade off. **Either format is appropriate for beginners in FB, unlike fantasy football where I recommend H2H due to the short (16 game) season.**

Finally, there is **Points-Based scoring**. This system is the most similar to fantasy football. Points are assigned to each statistical category. For example, four points for a HR and 1 point for a RBI. Overall standings are based on the total number of points for each category added together. Some leagues take it one step further and use points-based scoring for a H2H league.

There are three main variations of H2H. H2H (Points) was mentioned previously. In this scenario, points are assigned for each category and the team with the most total points wins the match up. The results from the H2H (Point) match up can be a win (1-0-0), loss (0-1-0) or tie (0-0-1). All three of the H2H variations allow team schedules, divisions and playoffs.

H2H (Each Category) is the most common variation. In this case, each category is won, lost or tied. If at the end of the H2H period, your team has 12 HRs and your opponent only has 10, you get a win for that category. In a 10-category league, the possible outcome could be anything from 0-0-10 to 10-0-0.

The last variation is H2H (Most Categories). With this variation, the team with the most category wins gets an overall win. The result of your H2H match up is simply a win, loss or tie. So one team will get a win and the other a loss, or both will tie. As opposed to H2H (Each Category) where you get a win for each category you beat your opponent.

Weekly or Daily Lineup

Some leagues set a lineup every day, others every week. Weekly lineups are generally set on Sunday night for the week ahead. One argument against a weekly lineup is that owners miss the nuances of daily game injuries, substitutions, suspensions, etc. An example of this is the All Star break. During the week of the MLB All Star game players have Monday through Wednesday off (the All Stars play Tuesday night) then games resume on Thursday. If you were playing in a weekly H2H league, you only have 4 games that week to compete. In many cases some of your pitchers will not play for you that week.

> The winning league in the All Star game earns home field advantage in the World Series that year. Thus the National league's win in 2010 means the NL team has the opportunity to play 4 of the possible 7 games of the World Series at home.
>
> There are 1200 players in MLB but only 68 are All Stars in any given year.

Draft type: Traditional or Auction

The traditional draft is sometimes called a serpentine draft since it reverses order every round, much like a snake doubling back on itself. In a traditional draft with a 12-team league, the first round goes in order 1 through 12, the second round then reverses as the 12th team gets to draft first and the 1st team (from round one) will draft last. Therefore, a five round draft would look like this:

Round 1: 1-12
Round 2: 12-1
Round 3: 1-12
Round 4: 12-1
Round 5: 1-12

Every odd numbered round (1st, 3rd, 5th and so on) has the order going from the team with the first 1st pick to the team with the 12th pick. Every even numbered round (2nd, 4th, 6th, etc.) will have the team with the 12th pick drafting first, then the 11th pick and so on until the 1st pick drafts last.

There are some disadvantages with this traditional draft format. If you have a later draft spot, you are not afforded an opportunity early to draft the most wanted players. If everyone agrees that Albert Pujols (1B, St. Louis Cardinals) is the most desirable player, there is little hope of him being available to later drafters, since the first or second owner drafting will inevitably draft him. However, since the draft "snakes," an owner with a later draft spot does get two picks before the owner with the higher draft spot gets his second pick, thus compensating them somewhat for their late start. The 12th spot has as much as a 5% disadvantage from the 1st spot and therefore I advocate alternatives to the traditional draft. For a detailed discussion of these alternate drafts, see *Fantasy Football Guidebook*.

An auction draft removes the biases of draft spot inequality. However, there are so few opportunities to participate in an auction draft that the default is a traditional draft. In an auction draft, owners start with a hypothetical budget with which to "buy" players at a player auction. Typically, $260 is used. The owner that bids the most for a given player is awarded that player and his budget is reduced by that amount. Unlike the traditional draft, every owner has the same chance to acquire every player if they wish to spend the money on them. The advantages of the auction system in removing any draft spot bias are offset by the additional time it may take for an auction draft and the "fear" of doing an untraditional draft. Unlike fantasy football, more FB leagues use an auction format. **Due to the complexities of an auction draft, I recommend beginners play in traditional draft leagues if possible. If you do play in an auction league, see Chapter 13 Auctions.**

Number of Teams (8, 10, 12, 14, 16 or 18)

An even number of teams is desirable if in a H2H league. If you have an odd number, then one team will be without an opponent every week. An odd number of teams can be fixed by using a rotisserie or points-based (versus a H2H) system, or by averaging the scores for all teams and having the bye week team (team with no opponent for the week) play against that average.

Most leagues consist of 8-15 teams. Some do have 16 or more, but this is stretching it. When you begin to consider 16 teams, take into consideration the amount of players drafted and the limited supply of certain positions (C, RP, OF, etc.) with only 30 MLB teams (see Appendix B Supply and Demand Table). If your league will have 16 teams and requires each team to own two C and RP, then there will be none available to pick up in free agency. On the opposite end of the spectrum, you can form or play in a league with only eight teams, but these are too small to be competitive. In 8-team leagues, everyone has great pitchers and hitters, so it is less about skill in drafting and more about luck as to who gets hurt or escapes injuries. Ten teams is, realistically, the minimum number of teams.

More teams means less players available in free agency, which means a harder league. More teams also mean more money for the prize, but more competition. **For these reasons, I recommend a 10 or 12-team league for beginners. Avoid 8 or 16-team leagues. The former is too easy and the latter could be too hard for beginners.**

Skill Level

Often a league will be targeted towards a certain skill level. This is described as beginner, intermediate or experienced owners. **If you are a beginner, start in the easiest league you can find,**

as far as the other owners' experience. No need to be humiliated in your first year of playing FB simply because you played with very experienced owners who know much more about the hobby due to years of experience.

There may be some overlap between skill level and some of the other variables mentioned in this chapter. For example, a beginner's league may limit the number of players on a roster or that can start. An experienced league has far less structured rules and allows owners to employ any strategy they choose. By selecting a beginner league, you may get more of the beginner tips mentioned in this chapter. **Smaller rosters favor beginners** because you have less players to draft and more players available to fix mistakes and team needs from free agency. **Small starter requirements also favor beginners** as it means less decisions.

Playoff Format

Your choice for determining the league champion is no playoffs, a multi-week playoff or single championship week. If no playoffs are desired, then at the end of the regular season the team with the best winning percentage (H2H) or points (roto) wins the league championship. One advantage to having no playoffs is that the regular season can be played until the end of the MLB regular season. Another advantage of the no playoff system is that all of the teams in the league get to compete for the entire season.

If you do want some type of elimination playoffs, you need to determine how many teams you want in the postseason tournament. Playoffs can start as early as week 23 or as late as week 26. The advantage of a playoff format is the excitement and intensity of single elimination. I recommend at least four teams in the playoffs. But no more than 50% of the total number of teams, no need to be like the NBA. The downside is that owners who do not make the playoffs have little to play for (having a bonus for high points each week helps create motivation for such teams).

Usually 12-team leagues go with four playoff teams and have playoffs in weeks 23 and 24 with the championship decided between the top two teams in weeks 25 and 26 with a two week competition.

Prizes

Look at how the league awards prizes. How much of the entry fee remains after administration costs, such as league management service, draft board and trophies? **A good ROT is first place gets 50%, second place gets 25% and third place gets their entry fee back.** Avoid leagues that award prizes to too many places. The object is to win!

Some argue that prizes should be all or nothing. In this case, the champion would get all the prize money. Again, these leagues breed apathy when an owner is out of contention. **The best format for beginners is to award prizes for at least the top three finishers so that everyone stays competitive the longest.**

Specialty Leagues

There are many variations of FB leagues. One specialty league is a keeper or dynasty league. In these leagues, owners can keep some or all (dynasty) of their players from the past season. **Keeper/Dynasty leagues are tougher for beginners and should be avoided until you have more experience.** See Chapter 14 for more on these types of leagues.

Number of Leagues

It goes without saying that the more leagues you play in, the more time you will need to spend on each. Therefore **I recommend a beginner start with just one league their first season.** See if you like it and how much time you want to put into it. If you have played one year and want to expand into another league in your second year - go for it. However, do not join 10 leagues in your first year. You will spread yourself too thin and you will not play some of your teams as competitively as if you had stuck to one league.

Summary

Checklist for picking a league:

1) Start with a free or low cost league

2) Play in a public league unless you know those in the private league

3) Try to play in a traditional serpentine draft (not an auction) if possible

4) Try to play in a league with 10 or 12 teams (the more teams there are, the harder it is to add good players later)

5) 7) Start with a lower skill level league, if possible

6) Choose a league where the prizes are available to more than just the top team

7) Avoid specialty leagues (Keeper, Dynasty, Auction, etc.) as a beginner

Chapter 4 How Do the Rules Affect Me?

This chapter will provide a broad overview of some of the more popular FB rules. More detailed rules are covered in later chapters. Scoring, drafts, free agency and trades are just a few of the additional topics that will have rules governing them. Ultimately, you pick the rules you want to play by, simply by joining a league and thereby agreeing to abide by those rules.

The rules mentioned in this book, _Fantasy Baseball for Beginners_, are by no means the only version of FB. That is what makes this game/hobby so much fun. There is no right or wrong way to play it. There are no golden rules nor ancient royal society that decides what is official and what is not. You decide what league to play in and thus agree to the rules. You live by the rules, and you win or lose by the rules of the league(s) you choose to play in.

The rules, once set before the draft, should remain the same for the entire season. The worst thing that can happen is a rule change after the season has started, because that will affect owners after they have made decisions based on the former rules. Always check to see how easy it is for the rules to be changed. You do not want the rules to be changed until the end of the season.

Just like playing monopoly and buying the railroads and then finding out you cannot build hotels on them; you need to know the rules of your league so that you know what strategies can pay off. **Knowing your league's rules can be a big advantage.** It sounds easy and it is, but many owners do not know all the rules in the league. They may not realize all the ways a player can be kept if injured or they may not know that rosters can be any number of players from any position. Knowing the rules inside and out (or knowing where to find them) can be an easy advantage.

Mixed, NL or AL Only Leagues

Mixed leagues use players from the entire MLB system, both the NL and the AL. NL Only leagues allow you to draft players from the 16 teams in the NL only. AL Only leagues have even less players since you can only draft a player from one of the 14 teams that play in the AL. The AL has more elite pitchers and catchers but fewer great SS or 1B. The drafting strategy is different in these AL or NL only leagues. **I am opposed to AL or NL only leagues because you can lose a player if he is traded to the other league.** I do not like any situation that allows luck to play a hand in success or failure.

Why limit yourself to NL or AL only? Steve Wulf, a Sports Illustrated writer and Rotisserie League owner, claims that fantasy teams in these formats more accurately reflect the major leagues. I agree, as owners tend to have more middle relievers and lesser known fielders due to the approximately 50% less player pool. **I recommend beginners start in a mixed league because that will mean more choice and less precise research.**

Roster Size

The roster size is the total number of players on your fantasy team. In most leagues, the roster size is limited to an even number so that the draft can be an even number of rounds and thus not give any team an advantage (see Chapter 7 - Draft). This number determines how many rounds the draft will last. The larger the number of rounds, the longer the draft lasts and the bigger the fantasy team you manage.

The more players you own, the fewer players there will be available to choose from if you need to replace someone (and vice versa). This is also affected by how many teams are playing in the league. The more teams that play, the fewer players available after the draft (see Appendix B Fantasy Baseball Supply and Demand Table).

In general, plan to have five more players than you need to start. So, if you have to start 23 players, plan on a total roster of 28 players. Obviously, some leagues have a smaller number of bench players than five, and some have more, and this will affect the game's strategy. The more bench players, the more important the draft, since fewer players are available after the draft.

Roster size will have some affect on who to draft and when. How many players to draft from each position will be determined by how many you start and how many extra players you have on your bench.

For beginners I recommend leagues with smaller rosters, that way you can seek replacements if needed and your draft day prep is less, since there are fewer players to choose.

The number of players kept at each position will change based on where you are in the season and how strong (deep) you are at the position. For example, if you are strong in saves towards the end of the season, you may want to drop one of your RPs and add a player who can help in stolen bases. Likewise, late in the season if your sleeper C has not made it to the majors, drop him and add another player who can contribute to your team, since he is getting the plate appearances because his MLB team wants to see if he can play in the majors.

Lineup

Each owner is responsible for setting a lineup (also known as the starting roster). The lineup requirement is stipulated in the rules and should be the same for the entire season. Lineups usually contain 13 batters and 9 pitchers. Read your league rules now and see what the starting lineup has to be.

The starting lineup deadline is also important. Some leagues allow changes every day up until the start of the first game. H2H leagues only allow changes until the period starts. For example, in a weekly H2H league, once the week starts you may be limited to only a few lineup changes.

Some leagues have a corner infielder (CI) position and a middle infielder (MI) position. This is known as a "flex" position. It gives the owner the flexibility to start either a 2B or SS in the case of a MI. A CI can be either a 1B or 3B depending on whom he thinks will score more points.

Realize that changing the number of starters can also affect the relative value of that position. Some leagues require that only one C start, which decreases demand and thus increases supply. Still other leagues start 2 catchers. Some leagues only start 1 RP thus removing the need for all but the best RPs. Some leagues require that six OFs start, thus increasing demand for that position and increasing the relative value of an OF.

Many leagues have a starting lineup of two Cs, one 1B, 2B, SS, 3B, MI, CI, five OFs, one DH, seven SPs and three RPs.

You can expect to start 22 to 23 players. Leagues with flex players (MI and CI) are more difficult. **If possible, stick to a league without a flex as a beginner.**

Eligibility

This determines what position a player can start. **Players with more flexibility (positions available to play) are valuable.** Players with no position at all such as David Ortiz (BOS, DH) can start in only one spot in your lineup.

Players playing at a position for 20 or more games the previous year will be eligible for that same position next year. In the current year, 10 games qualify a player at a new position. Any of the three OF positions (RF, CF, LF) count towards the 10 games played in the OF. Pitchers use five start or eight relief appearances the previous year. To add a different pitching position in the current season requires three starts or five relief appearances.

Free Agency (FA) Rules

Free agency is the process of adding different players to your team after the initial draft. This "need" may arise because of injury, suspension, retirement, poor play or a logistical need due to the player being demoted to the minor league. There are at least four different FA methods that a league may use.

4 Ways of Dealing with FA/Waiver Wire

1) First come, first served (FCFS)

Literally, the first owner to ask for a player gets him. This benefits those who are watching baseball live when the injuries or stories occur. I have been in leagues where the backup who just came off the bench is picked up, while the starter walks off with a torn rotator cuff. That is the wireless internet for you. FCFS allows adds/drops at any time. It is a disadvantage to those of us who have to do things like cut the grass, or go to a child's recital, and cannot watch all the games. **Avoid leagues that are FCFS** since beginners will not benefit as much.

2) Waiver Wire based on Weekly Ranking

This is awarded based on rankings (also known as worst to first format). Any player dropped goes on a waiver wire for a minimum amount of time. During this time limit (waiver period) teams may put in a waiver request to claim them At the end of the waiver period (typically 2-3 days), any player who has been claimed by more than one team is awarded to the team with the worst record. As a tiebreaker, the player would go to the team with the lowest total FPs scored to date for the current season. The waiver wire ranking is adjusted each week based on record. Advantage: All owners have a chance to get a player who is suddenly now available due to another team dropping them. Disadvantage: It rewards owners who drafted poorly or who do not manage their team well. Thus, the 0-6 goofus has a great RP fall in his lap through no skill of his own. Penalizes winning teams.

3) Waiver wire based on draft spot

Same as #2 above, but the waiver priority starts out based on where you drafted, and once you claim a player you go to the bottom of the priority list. Thus, if you have the last pick in a 10-team draft, you would have the #1 priority for the first claim you made. However, once you make a claim, you then fall to #10 on the waiver wire priority list. Advantage: Rewards owners who got bad draft spots, does not reward bad drafters or bad managers of their teams.

4) Blind bidding

Each team starts with 1,000 free agent "dollars" in their free agent acquisition budget (FAAB) for the season. Teams bid on players weekly. No team knows the other's bids until the winning bids have been awarded. The team with the highest bid is awarded that player. The winning team's FAAB is reduced by the winning bid amount and a player must be dropped to make room for the new acquisition. Once a team's FAAB reaches zero, they cannot bid on players. Advantages: Fairest system. Disadvantages: Hard to run on your own, no game day injuries plan.

Some leagues have a transactions deadline for the season. After this time, no adds/drops or trades can be performed.

Trades

Some leagues use a trading deadline to prevent collusion. However, if used, the deadline must be early enough to stop teams that are out of contention from dumping (dropping really good players to affect the league), but late enough to allow teams to navigate call ups from the minor leagues. Week 20 (mid August) seems like a great choice.

Some leagues rely on the commissioner's approval of trades; others rely on owners to vote to approve trades or veto trades (certain number vetoing = trade not put through); other leagues have an early trading deadline to prevent collusion for a playoff push. **Avoid leagues with trades, if possible.** If playing in a league that allows trades, try to keep the commissioner out of the business of approving trades. Make it an owner's vote (See Chapter Eleven – Trades for a detailed explanation of trades).

Summary

1) Know the rules of your league (and how to take advantage of them).
2) Avoid NL and AL only leagues if possible.
3) A league with smaller rosters is better for beginners because it requires less draft preparation (you draft fewer total players so your rankings do not have to be as comprehensive).
4) Leagues with smaller rosters also mean a more abundant supply of free agents to choose from, thus making a replacement choice easier.
5) Avoid leagues that use FCFS free agency.
6) Avoid the harder lineup decisions involved with flex positions.

Chapter 5 What are the Scoring Rules?

The players on your FB team accumulate statistics based on scoring categories. These categories are divided into two general positions: batting categories and pitching categories. If you elect to start a player, their statistics count towards your fantasy team. If the player is on your bench (you did not elect to start him) then the statistics for that day do NOT count toward your team's score. The number of points they get for each action or your team gets for each category is determined by the league's scoring system.

Often what sets a league apart from another league is the scoring system it implements. For some leagues this has been a lifelong pursuit, with growing pains and yearly tweaking to get it exactly right for the owners. Other leagues picked a system early on and have never changed it. **The bottom line is that you want the league to be fun and if it is not fun because of the scoring system, do not play in it.** MLB tracks, and makes available to the public, endless categories of statistics from each game. This opens up limitless possibilities for scoring rules. No rule is wrong, some are just better than others are for certain leagues and certain owners.

Before I get into the nuances of scoring categories, I want to start with one basic difference between FB leagues. In most instances, leagues can be broken down into the number of categories they use for scoring. The traditional league is an 8-category league, also known as a 4 x 4 league. 4 x 4 refers to the number of batting and pitching categories. The traditional format has four categories from batting and pitching. The original Rotisserie League formed by Dan Okrent was a 4 x 4 league, which used batting average, HRs, RBIs, SBs, wins, saves, ERA and WHIP as the eight scoring categories.

The other popular option is a 10-catgory league, also known as a 5 x 5 league. This league has five batting and five pitching categories. These leagues often add runs scored (R) for their extra hitting category and strikeouts (K) as the additional pitching category. I have played in both and believe that the 5 x 5 league represents MLB the best. Lead off hitters get the most runs scored since they bat the most and their job is to get on base. Pitchers who strike out the most batters tend to be the real workhorses on a staff. Both players lose too much value in a 4 x 4 league. **I recommend a 5 x 5 league for all FB owners.** All discussions from now on will assume a 5 x 5 league unless specified. If you see the term "in standard leagues" it usually refers to a 5 x 5 league using BA, R, HR, RBI, SB, ERA, WHIP, K, S and W.

Below are examples of the final results from a typical fantasy baseball league. The first table is the actual stats, the second is the points awarded and the third is the standings.

Scoring example (Final statistics)

	BA	R	RBI	HR	SB	W	S	K	ERA	WHIP
Team 1	.283	825	884	241	99	85	146	1226	3.70	1.26
Team 2	.276	835	798	201	120	81	143	1285	3.58	1.26
Team 3	.277	816	850	225	60	101	116	1119	3.64	1.24
Team 4	.266	817	669	163	160	103	6	1285	3.46	1.22
Team 5	.277	764	628	117	212	90	71	1195	3.42	1.19
Team 6	.275	856	869	231	119	71	75	1204	3.75	1.31
Team 7	.255	792	769	167	109	81	46	1184	3.38	1.21
Team 8	.274	825	664	150	109	99	54	1141	3.61	1.26
Team 9	.280	787	757	205	121	81	1	879	4.01	1.27
Team 10	.264	701	788	175	63	87	53	922	3.48	1.26
Team 11	.276	761	764	191	68	81	99	1122	3.71	1.32
Team 12	.270	774	704	193	155	62	157	852	3.93	1.35

Scoring example (Fantasy Points awarded per category to each team)

	BA	R	RBI	HR	SB	W	S	K	ERA	WHIP
Team 1	12	9.5	12	12	4	7	11	10	5	6.5
Team 2	7.5	11	9	8	8	4.5	10	11.5	8	6.5
Team 3	9.5	7	10	10	1	11	9	4	6	9
Team 4	3	8	3	3	11	12	2	11.5	10	10
Team 5	9.5	3	1	1	12	9	6	8	11	12
Team 6	6	12	11	11	7	2	7	9	3	3
Team 7	1	6	7	4	5.5	4.5	3	7	12	11
Team 8	5	9.5	2	2	5.5	10	5	6	7	6.5
Team 9	11	5	5	9	9	4.5	1	2	1	4
Team 10	2	1	8	5	2	8	4	3	9	6.5
Team 11	7.5	2	6	6	3	4.5	8	5	4	2
Team 12	1	1	1	7	10	1	12	1	2	1

Standings

	Points	Points Behind
Team 1	89	-------
Team 2	84	5
Team 3	76.5	12.5
Team 4	73.5	15.5
Team 5	72.5	16.5
Team 6	71	18
Team 7	61	28
Team 8	58.5	30.5

Team 9	51.5	37.5
Team 10	48.5	40.5
Team 11	48	41
Team 12	46	43

Scoring Categories

The categories a league uses will determine your overall strategy in many ways because not all leagues use the same categories. Make sure the league has the same number of batting and pitching categories. If not, the area that has the most categories should be weighted more in your draft preparations.

Fielding categories are available for things such as errors, double plays turned, outfield assists and putouts. **However, I do not recommend fielding categories as too much luck is introduced by their use.** The most common batting and pitching categories are:

Batting	Pitching
Runs Scored (R)	Wins (W)
Home Runs (HR)	Saves (S)
Runs Batted In (RBI)	Strikeouts (K)
Stolen Bases (SB)	Earned Run Average (ERA)*
Batting Average (AVG)	Walks plus Hits Per Innings Pitched (WHIP)*

* Indicates a category where the lower the number the better ranking.

What are these categories and how are they calculated?
Is there a strategy to use for each?

Batting Categories

Runs Scored (R)

A player who advances around all the bases to score is credited with a run or run scored. The player must get on base first. Good base running skills often help advance to additional bases. Of course, the hitters who bat behind him will also determine how many runs a player can score. **Players who are walked often have more runs scored but may lose RBI opportunities.** Leadoff hitters should score the most runs since they bat first and are given this responsibility due to their ability to get on base. This is a very MLB team-dependent statistic.

Home Runs (HR)

When a batter circles all the bases and touches home plate in one play without any errors committed by fielders.

Runs Batted In (RBI)

Number of runners who scored due to batter's action except if an error is committed or he hit into a double play. RBIs depend on players ahead of you getting on base. Generally, the third, fourth and fifth batters have more RBIs.

Stolen Bases (SB)

Number of bases advanced other than on batted balls, walks or hits by pitch.

> Note: If a player steals a base but the catcher does not throw because it is insignificant (player steals 2B, but there is a runner on 3B), this is called defensive indifference and the player does not get a SB awarded.

In real life, you need to steal three bases for every time you are caught stealing (CS). This is because the loss of a base runner and the out it creates are so harmful to a MLB team scoring. So unless the player is good at base stealing, he is rarely sent. Traditionally,

BOS and OAK are teams who do not steal much. **In FB, because SB is one of the five batting categories and they are rare; it makes SBs more valuable.**

Batting Average (AVG)

Hits divided by at-bats. Unfortunately, luck plays too important a role in a player's BA. The difference between a hit and an out is often determined by other events. Did the bloop single or ground ball find a hole? Was the 2B moving to cover a possible steal attempt? What I am saying is that hitters go in slumps and often it is not that he is not hitting the ball (making contact) but instead just hitting it hard at the wrong place and time.

If a hitter is a career .300 hitter, but is batting .250, is he in a slump or just unlucky? **Contact rate (at bats-strikeouts/at bats) is a better measure of the hitter's difficulties.** The league average for contact rate is about 80%. Hitters batting .300 generally have a contact rate of 90% and .250 hitters have a 70% contact rate. If the player in question had his contact rate drop from 90 to 75%, then I would say he has lost some of his ability to hit. If the contact rate is essentially the same then the same player is probably just a victim of some bad luck.

Look for players with high contact rates. Anytime you make more contact you have a 30% chance of a hit, more contact means more hits. A strikeout is an out every time. A ball that is hit can be a hit or an out or force an error.

Pitching Categories

Pitching statistics for pitchers are affected by the team they play on. The fielders playing behind the pitcher will determine how many runs are scored, in some cases based on errors or superior play. The parks where a pitcher pitches can also affect these categories.

Wins (W)

Number of times a pitcher was pitching when his team took the lead and the other team never exceeded the runs scored for him. Twice in the past four years no pitcher has had 20 or more wins.

It is my firm belief that wins should not be used in FB. Often it is beyond a pitcher's control whether he wins or loses a game. Run support from your own batters influences the win or loss more than I care to think about. The exact opposite can occur too, benefiting your opponent's pitcher's weak performance. And what about bullpen support or lack thereof? There are few things worse than having your pitcher leave with a 3-1 lead in the eighth inning and watching helplessly as the set up man gives up a walk and a 2 run homer. **SP on teams with weak bullpens will have fewer wins.** The poster child for not using wins is Ben Sheets in 2004. Pitching for the Milwaukee Brewers that year, Ben was in the top in ERA (2.70) and WHIP (0.98). His strikeout to walk ratio was an astounding 8:1. His win-loss record? 12-14. With an ERA of 2.70. Quality starts (see below) is a better measure of a pitcher's worth.

Saves (S)

The rules are complicated for when a save is a save. Suffice it to say, relief pitchers known as closers get the save opportunities. Often a bad team can still have lots of saves. A strong team that blows away their opponents (ahead by more than four runs) late in the game do not provide as many save opportunities.

Strikeouts (K or SO)

Number of batters who received three strikes.

Earned Run Average (ERA)

Total number of earned runs multiplied by 9 and divided by innings pitched. A P who gives up 2 runs in 6 innings of work has a ERA for that game of $3.0 = (2 \times 9)/6$.

Walks plus Hits per Innings Pitched (WHIP)

Total number of walks and hits divided by the number of innings pitched. If a pitcher gives up 8 hits and 4 walks in 6 innings, his WHIP is 2.0 based on $8+4=12/6$.

Some better measures

I suggest looking for a league that uses OBP and SLG instead of HRs and BA. Likewise a league that uses QS instead if wins

On Base Percentage (OBP)

Hits plus walks plus hit by pitch divided by at-bats plus walks plus hit by pitch plus sacrifice flies. **Good measure of ability to get on base and score runs.**

$$OBS= \frac{H+BB+HBP}{AB+BB+HBP+SF}$$

Slugging Percentage or (SLG)

Also known by slugging average, SLG is total bases divided by at-bats. Total bases are 1 for a single, 2 for a double, 3 for a triple and 4 for a HR. **SLG is a measure of the power of a hitter.** Walks are excluded from this calculation. The maximum SLG is 4.0, but only for the hitter that hits a HR every at-bat.

$$SLG = \frac{(1B) + (2 \times 2B) + (3 \times 3B) + (4 \times HR)}{AB}$$

On Base Plus Slugging Percentage (OPS)

Add OBP and SLG to get OPS. **OPS represents the ability of a player to get on base and hit for power, perhaps the two most important hitting skills.** However, the OPS is different based on variables such as league playing in and the venue that a player plays in too. An OPS of .750 is representative of MLB with the best player near 1.00

On Base Percentage Against (OBA)

Measures a pitcher's ability to prevent hits or how does the league bat against the pitcher.

Quality Starts (QS)

Any game in which the pitcher pitches at least six innings and does not give up more than three earned runs. This helps alleviate some of the luck in how a pitcher's team supports him with runs. It is frustrating to see your pitcher pitch well (quality start) only to watch them lose because of a blown save or no run support and take the tough loss. By the same token, a cheap win can occur when your opponent's pitcher does not have a quality start (gives up six runs) yet gets a win because his team scored eight runs for him.

My only objection to QS is the complete game pitcher who gives up four runs, but does not get a QS because he gave up more than 3.0 earned runs. In reality, he could have had a better ERA for the game since the other pitcher could have left after six innings and 3.0 earned runs with a 4.5 ERA. I suggest allowing CG (Complete Game-pitchers who pitch all 9 innings) starters with a 4.0 or better ERA to qualify for a QS.

Losses (L)

Pitcher who allowed the opposing team to take the ultimate lead, never regained the lead and his team lost. I do not like losses for many of the same reasons I do not like wins. Quality starts is a better measure in my opinion. **Avoid leagues that use losses as a pitching category since they introduce more luck than skill in predicting player performance.**

I have written it before but will repeat it again (it is that important). **Know the rules of your league**. It can be a big advantage. Are pitchers penalized for losses? If yes, how much? Are pitchers awarded extra points for a CG? If yes, who gets those chances these days?

Summary

1) Make sure the league's scoring rules are fun. If they are too cumbersome, and you cannot understand how they are determined, avoid the league.

2) Play in a 5 x 5 league if possible.

3) However, I do not recommend fielding categories as too much luck is introduced by their use.

4) Saves and SB are the two rarest scoring categories.

5) In FB, because SB is one of the five batting categories and they are rare; it makes SBs more valuable.

6) SP on teams with weak bullpens will have fewer wins.

7) I suggest looking for a league that uses OBP and SLG instead of HRs and BA. Likewise a league that uses QS instead of wins.

8) Avoid leagues that use losses as a pitching category since they introduce more luck than skill in predicting player performance.

9) Know the rules of your league.

Chapter 6 How do I Rank Players (Positions)?

You need to identify the players who will score the most FPs. Later, Chapter 8 discusses ranking individual players by positions for a cheat sheet. This chapter will discuss player positions in general terms, so that you can understand the trends at each position. Finally, some common terms used in evaluating players are explained.

How many do I rank at each position?

Tiers

A tier is a group of players you value the same. If faced with a choice between drafting any of them, you would not care who you drafted. Tiering protects you from yourself. Instead of reaching for a catcher too early, with a tier you can see that there are five others of the same value. Instead of drafting the C too early, you can draft the OF who is the last in his OF tier. Tiering helps owners recognize value in a draft.

There is no magic formula for how many players can be in a given tier, nor how many tiers a position will have. In 2010, Hanley Ramirez (FLA, 3B) was the only player in my top 3B tier. Contrast that with four players in my 2nd 1B tier. I have had as many as eight tiers at OF and four at C some years. A good average is about six tiers (seven if there is just one top stud who takes a tier all to themselves-think Albert Pujols, STL, 1B). Remember there should be a significant gap between players from one tier to the next. I call these gaps "talent drops". If you are in an auction, $6 increments works well as tier levels. For example, all players $19-$25 in the same tier.

Hitting

As discussed earlier look at contact rate.
Also look at the ratio of BB to K. A BB/K ratio of 3.5 is average.
4.0 or better reflects good plate discipline. Remember every walk
leads to run scored opportunities and a better OPS.

**Remember players who walk often are laggards in the HR and
RBI categories generally due to fewer opportunities.**

Hitters tend to peak around age 27 (catchers a few years later).
Hitters who strikeout 1/3 of the time do not become .300 hitters.

**Look for power and plate discipline with stolen base ability a
distant third. Repeat after me "Power over Speed."**

Look for OBP over .350 (above .300 is OK)
SLG over .440 (above .400 a must)

Position Data

First Baseman (1B)

1B tend to be tall, quick-reflexed and very flexible as they are
responsible for catching the balls thrown from the other infielders
on a ground ball. Often balls hit towards first base are hit harder
than middle infield hits. It is common for veteran players to move
to 1B later in their career to extend it due to the perceived lower
range of movement at the position. Granted 1B do hold runners on
base more often and the position can be less physically demanding.
This also means 1B are least likely to become injured.

Second Baseman (2B)

2B need to be quick and smart as they are the field general and the key to critical double plays. Speed and a good arm are attributes of a good 2B. However, these attributes do not bode well for power hitting. Do not expect too many HRs from 2B.

Short Stop (SS)

SS is the most dynamic position in baseball. Most hitters are right-handed and many pull the ball slightly, thus giving the SS more of the fielding responsibilities. Due to his location, the SS needs one of the strongest arms on the field and is primarily a right-handed player. Thus, he can make throws to either first or second base without having to pivot after catching the ball. Traditionally, SS has been a weak hitter's position, but recent years have seen this trend change.

Third Baseman (3B)

3B is called the "hot corner" due to the speed of the balls hit there and the fact that 3B are closer to the batters who hit primarily to the right. 3B must have strong arms since they will inevitably throw the furthest to get to 1B. The position is known for power hitting, yet fewer 3B are in the Hall of Fame than any other position.

Catcher (C)

Catchers are involved in every defensive play on the ball field; because of this they are susceptible to injury more than in other positions. Their hitting deficiencies are also overlooked if their catching skills are good enough. Do not draft a catcher early. Wait on them. They do not have good statistics and often miss games due to injury, rest required or pitcher preferences. Injuries include knee issues and assorted ailments resulting from catching a 95 MPH ball over and over, night after night. Larger and heavier C tend to have more problems and regardless of the size C often have games off to recover.

Outfielder (OF)

OF in general tend to be power hitters (especially LF and RF). OF also do not have as much involvement in fielding plays and thus can be less prone to some injuries. However, the speed with which the OF attacks fly balls and the constant threat of hitting a OF fence always make an injury a worry. CF tends to be the fastest and best athlete as they must back up the other OF. CF also tend to be lead off batters on a team due to their speed. RF will have the better arm since they need to make the throws to third base and home plate. In many leagues, OF is the scarcest position in terms of starting MLB players and fantasy roster spots (see Appendix B).

Pitching

For any batting appearance, there are three possible outcomes: walk, strikeout, and ball in play. **Thirty percent of balls in play are hits**. However, of those balls in play, 46% are ground balls and 54% are fly balls (includes line drives). Ground balls rarely are HRs (the exception being the inside the park home run). Fly balls are HRs 7% of the time. So, ground ball pitchers have a huge advantage in NOT allowing as many HRs. **Pitchers who do not allow HRs or walks are the best pitchers and have the lowest ERA.**

Pitchers with high strikeouts have fewer balls in play. This means fewer hits (typically 2 less hits per 9 innings). Fewer hits mean fewer base runners and a lower ERA. It also means a lower WHIP. A pitcher's command is determined by his strikeouts and walks. Strikeouts show movement and speed control. Walks are an indication of poor location of pitches. **Walks are ERA killers**. Pitchers who give up a lead off walk end up giving up one or more runs that inning much of the time.

Any runner on base, whether from a walk, hit or being hit by a pitch, means a better chance for an opposing team to score. A HR with no runner on base only costs one run. But with runners on base, everyone scores.

Pitcher Analysis

1) K/BB ratio

    a. 2.0 is as low as a good pitcher can allow

    b. 2.5 is what you should search for in a pitcher

    c. 3.0 Grab him immediately

    d. Remember a high strikeout pitcher can allow more walks so focus on this ratio not the total number of walks

2) HR ratio (HR/9 Innings)

    a. The HR average for batters is 4%. For every plate appearance minus BB, K, HBP and sacrifice bunts (balls in play) there are 1 out of 25 HRs.
Therefore, a little over 1 HR per 9 innings is average

    b. Look for pitchers with a HR ratio of 1.25 or less

    c. Evaluate further pitchers with a HR ratio of 1.5 or more

3) Ground ball ratio (GB/Balls in play or sometimes seen as GB/FB ratio expressed as 2.5 etc-but this does not include line drives which is misleading)

    a. A GB ratio of 45% is average

    b. Look for a GB ratio of 50% or greater

Typical ground ball pitchers: Brandon Webb, Felix Hernandez or Aaron Cook

4) K/IP

    a. .667 is a good strikeout ratio (2 K every 3 IP)

5) Look for pitchers age 25-29

    a. Pitchers tend to peak at age 30

    b. Young pitchers (below age 25) are OK if they came into the league at an early age and have some experience.

Pitchers that are "ground ball" pitchers throw more pitches low in the bottom of the strike zone. If you keep the ball down you will induce ground balls and more double plays if runners are on base. 6.5% of all eligible ground balls are converted into double plays.

Starting Pitcher (SP)

Most injury prone position in MLB; hence the usual 70/30 split in auctions between hitter and pitcher budgets. Look at WHIP as it is a great measure of a pitcher's ability to prevent hitters from reaching base. If you give up a lead off walk or hit, it often leads to a run. Avoid "Innings eaters"-pitchers who pitch 200 innings with a low K rate (think WAS, SP Livan Hernandez). These guys kill you in ERA and WHIP while not even denting Ks.

As mentioned earlier, do not worry too much about Wins and ERA. Both are very unpredictable in many respects. Run support and bullpen support are the two biggest factors other than the pitcher's ability, which can affect performance in terms of W and ERA.

Rookie pitchers are least productive (Strasburg is the exception to this rule). Second year pitchers are next least productive. You can see where this is going. Look for a P with at least two or more years of experience.

Look at the run support a pitcher received the year before and evaluate what kind of run support he may expect in the coming year. A change of team or key players on the same team can influence the run support he gets. **Wins are highly correlated to ERA and run support. Avoid P with a 4.25 or higher ERA or a 1.5 or higher WHIP.**

Relief Pitcher (RP)

Saves are the most overrated statistic in FB. **Owners forget that closers on bad teams get tons of opportunities too.** Matt Capps, WAS, RP, is leading MLB in saves as I write this just before the All-Star break. Bad teams (yes Nationals I mean you) often win by fewer than three runs. So unlike the New York Yankees who blow teams away, Washington, when they win, win close games that need a closer.

Opportunity is the key. If the pitcher is not put into the close situation he cannot get the save. There are only 30 closers and some of them will not be closers by the All-Star break. Statistically, nearly 40% of the opening day closers are not finishing by season end. Some of the elite closers are always there (Mariano Rivera, NYY,

RP). Break down the closers into categories based on their job situation. If their position is the least bit shaky, know who could replace them. Rank them based on job security. **The least stable should be last in your rankings** and their possible replacements should be next in the rankings after the first 30.

NEVER use a rookie closer.

What does it take to win?

In a typical 5 x 5 league with 12 teams using the standard scoring system, the following statistics won these categories (23 starters-14 batters/9 pitchers (7 SP/2 RP).

HITTERS		PITCHERS	
R	1200	W	100
HR	225	SV	130
RBI	1100	K	1500
SB	200	ERA	3.30
BA	.285	WHIP	1.15

In the same format as above but with 15 teams (National Fantasy Baseball Championship-NFBC) using the standard scoring system, the following statistics won these categories (23 starters-14 batters/9 pitchers (7 SP/2 RP).

HITTERS		PITCHERS	
R	**1070**	W	110
HR	270	**SV**	**95**
RBI	**1000**	K	1500
SB	200	ERA	3.30
BA	.285	WHIP	1.15

Note the reduced statistics in bold. In the high stakes NFBC, a greater number of teams mean less top numbers in R, RBI and SV. However, averages like BA, ERA and WHIP remain unchanged.

Risky/Breakdown Players

Breakdown players are players who are past their prime and have a greater chance of injury or benching due to poor performance.

What is poor performance? As far as pitchers, the average for a SP is 28 GS, 170 IP, 11-10 record, 4.10 ERA, 1.33 WHIP and 132 K. For a RP it is 66 IP, 4-4 record, 15 saves, 3.4 ERA, 1.25 WHIP and 65 K. So RP have a better ERA and WHIP.

The hitting averages depend on fielding positions. The average player has 420 AB, 114 H, 14 HR, 60 R, 57 RBI, 8 SB and a .272 AVG. Catchers have much less at 370 AB, 46 R, 52 RBI, 2 SB and a .263 AVG. OF are more avg, 1B and 3B is generally stronger and 2B and SS worse than average.

Who is a Stud?

Your top 3-4 draft picks are your studs (your 4 best players). All players who are ranked in the top 5 at any position are studs. You may even get a stud with your 4th draft pick, if drafting from the back end of the draft (picks 8-12). Why do you care who is a stud? **Never bench a stud unless he is hurt or benched (see Rule #3 Chapter 9).**

Who is a Sleeper?

A sleeper is someone who is relatively unknown and who performs much better than expected, based on his draft position. Think of them as something that may prove valuable that no one else may know about. You want to get them, but not too early and sacrifice a known player who could help your team. Sleepers give you a chance to break away from the other teams if they perform well. This sets you apart and gives you a better chance of winning a championship. Many times I have seen an owner draft well but never gamble on a sleeper or two. This owner only makes the playoffs half of the time and never understands why I always make the playoffs. It is because I take a few chances, and when they pan out it means I have a great player that no one expected. The sleeper who hits (performs well) gives me the extra edge I need to make the playoffs. The trick is finding the sleepers.

The key is to have at least five sleeper picks ranked in order of expected draft position (i.e. ADP-average draft position-which round you think other owners will draft them if given the chance). That way when someone steals a sleeper or two it will not destroy your whole sleeper plan. Having just two or three sleepers and seeing them taken before you can pull the trigger is a bit demoralizing. Of course, the later the round you take a sleeper, the more the payoff if he performs (because hopefully you picked someone with value ahead of him, rather than grabbing your sleeper a round earlier). **Sleepers are best in the OF.** Even if he turns out to be a bust, you have not hurt yourself since the position is so deep.

Tips for Picking Sleepers

1)   Look for a window of opportunity. Remember Skill+Opportunity = Success. Does the starter have injury problems, contractual issues, off-the-field problems, hitting/fielding problems? Is there a new coach to get used to? Did the team add/lose another player (add stud SP/ lose RP) who can help?

2)   More sleepers are of the young variety than the old variety. **Look at 2nd or 3rd year players** simply because they have had time to learn their systems and make the rookie mistakes. **You are more likely to find a sleeper in someone who has not been in the league more than four or five years.** If they have been playing longer, then they have had their chance and it probably has passed them by. There are exceptions to this, but for the most part go with youth for sleepers.

OF makes the best candidates for sleepers so look for:

1) Look for players in their 2nd-5th year (who are 1st round MLB picks)

2) Rookie players rarely (5% of the time) breakout. A breakout season occurs when a player greatly exceeds expectations. Rookies who do well in their first year tend to breakout the next year.

3) Look for dedication to the craft. Look for the player who arrives early and stays late; the ones who practice in the off-season or take extra time before every game to practice with their

hitting or pitching coach. These are the ones who will provide consistent performance.

Draft Steals and Busts

Here are some terms owners use to describe potential players in the draft. What is a "**steal**" in the draft? Any player drafted two or more rounds below where he finished in the end of season rankings based on total fantasy points is a steal. If I drafted a SS in the 5th round with the 53rd pick (5.05) and he finishes 24 places higher or more, then he was a steal (29th overall in points scored; 3rd round, 5th pick).

A player who performs one round better than where he was picked would be considered a **good pick**. Again, in a 12-team league that would be a player who finishes 12 spots higher in the rankings than his pick.

An early (**reach**) pick would be a player who finishes a round further down the rankings.

A **bust** would be a player who finishes more than two rounds lower than he was drafted.

Summary

1) Use tiers
2) Look for power and plate discipline with speed a distant third
3) Wait on catcher-they are hurt more often
4) Target a SP with a high K to BB ratio
5) Avoid P with a 4.25 or higher ERA or a 1.5 or higher WHIP
6) Saves can come from bad teams
7) Sleepers are best from the OF
8) You are more likely to find a sleeper in someone who has not been in the league more than four or five years

Chapter 7 When/where/how/how long is the Draft?

The draft is like Christmas day, some even call it "Christmas in March". You have your eyes on something special and you hope you get it. The anticipation of the event building up in the weeks before is tremendous. You lose sleep the night before. On draft day you are like a kid wondering what you are going to get. Draft day can be that exciting!

Drafts can be live, online or over the phone. If the owners cannot be physically present then the draft is conducted automatically online. Live drafts are the most fun. Online drafts are more convenient but less fun. Automatic online drafts are about as fun as watching paint dry.

Draft Date

As a beginner, I recommend you try to draft as close to the start of the MLB season as possible. This way there are fewer questions about a team's starters. The ideal time for the draft would be the weekend before the MLB season starts. After spring training is over you should have a good idea of the starters on each team. The later it is (closer to MLB opening day), the more information you have to make informed choices. It will be a date that everyone can make. Usually this will mean a Saturday afternoon (especially if it is a live draft).

Live Draft Location

Any location that is quiet, large enough and easy to get to will work. Back yards and garages/basements work well. In many cases the draft will be at the home of the commissioner or some owner who volunteers his abode. **No matter where it is held, make sure you get a comfortable seat, that is quiet (not beside the kitchen or bathroom) and have room for your materials (cheat sheets, magazine, etc.).**

Think twice before offering to host the draft as a beginner. The owner of the draft house has some advantages and some disadvantages. The main advantage is the familiarity factor. He knows his house and will be comfortable in the surroundings. He will not have to drive to the draft so he can use the extra time saved (what would have been travel time to the draft) to prepare for the draft. And, perhaps most importantly, he can have the latest information from his computer right up until the other owners arrive.

The problems with being the host are the distractions that can occur if coordinating the party (food, beverages, etc.). On the day of the draft, some time will need to be spent arranging furniture and cleaning up before the guests arrive. Once the draft starts, as the host, it may be easy to get distracted by helping the guests with food, beverages, etc.

Many leagues have moved the draft (and thus the stress) out of private homes and into public places such as a bar, restaurant or conference room. If your draft is conducted at a public place, make sure you have some privacy and are not near the band, jukebox or television. Buffalo Wild Wings (BWW) Grill & Bar offers their restaurants as draft locations, along with offering free wings. It is an excellent place to hold a draft.

Online Drafts

In an online draft, owners draft from their own personal computers simultaneously. These drafts are held in your home office or wherever you wish to have your computer. The same rules apply as the live draft: Minimize distractions, make the room quiet and have another computer as a backup in case the primary computer has issues. For the same reasons, **always pre-rank your players for the online draft before the draft,** that way if you get disconnected for some reason, the computer's artificial intelligence (AI) will draft players you want and not players the AI thinks you want. Often the league's initial rankings have retired, injured and suspended players ranked inappropriately.

Draft Rules

All of the draft rules below should be covered in the league constitution. Make sure that all draft rules are in writing and that you have a copy two weeks before draft day. If you have a question on a rule, ask before the draft in order to get it cleared up early. **Know all the draft rules and the penalties for violating them.** Some leagues charge money, ask you to buy a round of drinks, or penalize your team with a later draft pick if you violate a draft rule. **Sometimes the penalty is so light that violating a rule may be worth the punishment.**

Ask the commissioner if this is a friendly league (usually it will be if no serious money is on the line) or a strict league. Often in a friendly league, allowances are made for new owners. However, you do not want to look like a rookie so read below and heed.

Who Can Be Drafted

Some leagues allow any player to be drafted; others wait until a player is called up to the majors before making them eligible. Still other leagues insist only that the player has played one game of MLB. This prevents college players from being taken before they play MLB but does not prevent you from drafting unemployed or retired players who may make a comeback. Know your league rules. A hot prospect in the minor leagues may be worth a late round draft pick.

Time Limits

What about time limits to make picks? Anywhere from 1-2 minutes is normal, with 90 seconds as the most common. Don't panic! This is more than enough time if you are prepared…and you will be prepared if you follow the basic instructions outlined here. Some leagues use a clock (www.draftclock.com) and give a 30-second and 10-second warning before time expires. Some leagues allow less time for the first half of the draft (as an example, one minute since it is easier to make picks) and more time for the second half of the draft (possibly two minutes).

Keep in mind that the longer the time limit the longer it will take to finish the draft. For example, a 12-team league with 25 rounds would equal 300 picks. If two minutes were allowed per pick, theoretically you could be drafting for 600 minutes or 10 hours. Most players do not take the full time, but some do and all can if they want. **A 12-team, experienced league with 25 rounds, utilizing the one and two minute time limit in the example above, can finish their draft in approximately five hours.**

What if I Miss My Pick?

Normally, if an owner does not make a pick in the time allotted, he skips his pick until the next owner drafts. Therefore, you just have to wait one pick before you get another chance at drafting. However, the time allowed for this "makeup pick" is usually only 5-10 seconds. So be ready to go when the owner after you drafts. Each subsequent time you miss the deadline you will move back a slot and get five to ten seconds to pick. Once time expires, even if you blurt out a name, you forfeit your pick until the next owner makes his pick.

This happens when you only have one player in mind to pick next and the owner just ahead of you drafts him-doh! **The best way to avoid this is to have 2-3 players ready to draft when your turn comes around.**

What if I Pick a Player Already Chosen?

If an owner selects a player already drafted or violates the roster limits with his pick (such as maximum of three RPs and he drafts a fourth) he may be penalized. The penalty can be monetary or otherwise, or just a warning. A common penalty is deferment of their draft pick. In a friendly league, a good-natured ribbing is the worst you may expect.

Other Draft Considerations

Find out what colors the stickers are for each position on the draft board in advance of the draft. Some programs for ranking players allow you to customize the colors used for positions, thus giving you a jump ahead of the competition since the cheat sheet matches the colors on the draft board.

Draft Format

There are two main formats for the draft order. They are the serpentine method and the standard method. The standard method is used in specialty leagues like keeper/dynasty leagues.

Most drafts will use a serpentine method. In serpentine, the draft order reverses ("snakes back") on successive rounds. The first round would be picks 1-12, in that order. The second round would go in reverse order. Team 12 would get the first pick in round two and Team 1 (who picked first in round one) would get the last pick. Team 1 gets back-to back picks for every pick except the first and last rounds. Team 12 (or the last team in the draft) always has back-to-back picks. Odd rounds comply with the original draft order (1-12) and even rounds are the reverse (12-1). Therefore, the first four rounds would look like this: 1-12; 12-1; 1-12; 12-1. Know when your draft pick is and how many other picks are between your picks (see the chart below). **The closer you are to the first or last draft spots, the less time you have between picks.**

Pick 1	Overall picks 1, 24, 25, 48	23/1 between picks
Pick 2	Overall picks 2, 23, 26, 47	21/3 between picks
Pick 3	Overall picks 3, 22, 27, 46	19/5 between picks
Pick 4	Overall picks 4, 21, 28, 45	17/7 between picks
Pick 5	Overall picks 5, 20, 29, 44	15/9 between picks
Pick 6	Overall picks 6, 19, 30, 43	13/11 between picks
Pick 7	Overall picks 7, 18, 31, 42	11/13 between picks
Pick 8	Overall picks 8, 17, 32, 41	9/15 between picks
Pick 9	Overall picks 9, 16, 33, 40	7/17 between picks
Pick 10	Overall picks 10, 15, 34, 39	5/19 between picks
Pick 11	Overall picks 11 14, 35, 38	3/21 between picks
Pick 12	Overall picks 12, 13, 36, 37	1/23 between picks

The other draft format is the standard draft order, which is what MLB uses. In this case, the same draft order repeats every round. For example, the first three rounds would be 1-12, 1-12 and 1-12. Drafts for MLB rookies in FB dynasty leagues use this format the most.

Draft Order-How Do I Know When I Pick?

Draft order can either be known well in advance or decided right before drafting on draft day. If the draft spots are to be known in advance, they can either be ordained by the rules (reverse order of finish from last year) or drawn at random. Leagues that use the reverse order of finish for a draft order will have the order known at the end of the season. In most cases, a new owner will be allowed to draft first. These teams will have over six months to mull over their draft spot and the strategies that go with it. It also allows more time to think about trading draft picks. If you wish to trade a draft pick, review trading in Chapter 11.

Picking draft spots at the actual draft eliminates these advantages. However, if your league waits until draft day, when everyone is present (by drawing numbers or cards out of a hat), it is hard to be challenged as to the fairness of who got what pick. It also prevents the owner who gets the last draft pick from deciding to quit (since he is drafting last and hates his draft spot). **Try to play in a league where your draft spot will be known in advance. That way you can practice (mock draft) from that spot before the actual draft (see Chapter 8).**

Draft Day Experience

If possible, volunteer to assist with a draft before you actually draft in one. Many leagues have someone else place the labels on the board. You can ask to be this person. Placing the labels is a great way to learn some of the MLB players, teams and positions. You may have done this last year and seen how much fun the draft was and decided to join that same league this year.

Making Sure You Get the Right Player

Unfortunately, there are several Andersons (6), Bakers (3), Molinas (3), Johnsons (9), and Escobars (3) in MLB right now. So, knowing a player's last name is not enough to guarantee you get the right player. **Make sure you have the correct name and announce his full name, position and team to avoid any controversy.** You do not have to pronounce the players name correctly, but you must get it close. If you do not do this correctly, you could be stuck with Jose Molina, Tampa Devil Ray catcher instead of the better catcher Yadier Molina, of St. Louis Cardinals fame.

Intermission

A draft can take four or more hours and thus at least one break is recommended. As a beginner, push for as many intermissions (10-15 minute breaks) as possible because it gives you time to recover and catch up with the draft if you fall behind. Use breaks to your advantage by updating your cheat sheets (See Appendix G Cheat Sheet Sample), mapping out strategies or examining team strengths or weaknesses. A ten-minute break in the middle to let everyone go to the bathroom seems fair. Know when the breaks are coming and do not let others push for "pressing on." Take the break to catch your breath since as a beginner you are probably farther behind than other owners are.

Summary

1. Make Draft day as close to the start of the MLB season as possible to eliminate unknowns such as starters, injuries, etc.
2. Get a comfortable draft seat. Avoid distractions at the draft such as food, noise, alcohol or visual distractions.
3. Know all the draft rules and penalties.
4. Find out your draft spot before the draft and practice (mock draft-see Chapter 8 Draft Preparation).
5. Announce the correct player's full name, position and NFL team to avoid drafting the wrong Johnson or Molina.
6. Ask for as many draft intermissions ("breaks") as possible. It helps beginners catch their breath and update their materials.

Chapter 8 How Do I Prepare for the Draft?

There are four major steps to draft preparation. First, you must decide on a draft strategy. This is your plan for the draft, in essence, it is what position to pick, who to pick and when to pick them. To execute this plan you will need a ranking of players at each position and an overall ranking or evaluation system. These rankings are commonly called cheat sheets (See Appendix G Cheat Sheet Sample). Next, create or procure a cheat sheet for your draft. Third, you must gather your draft materials together. No, it is not just your cheat sheets but also much more. Finally, practice drafting as much as possible to get a feel for how it happens.

Draft Strategy (Have a Plan)

There is an old saying that goes "If you fail to prepare, you prepare to fail." Have a plan. Who do I draft and when? This plan will be based on your draft strategy. There are several strategies from which to choose. Remember any of the strategies can be winners depending on the league. If there was one best way to draft everyone would do it that way.

The key to a draft strategy is flexibility. All of the strategies can work in certain draft situations. All can fail in certain other situations. If you are in an auction or keeper draft, some work better than others do. Sometimes you may have to change or combine strategies in the middle of a draft. Knowing the advantages and disadvantages of each will help with those draft decisions.

Draft Strategies

Position Scarcity Strategy-

Try to get players at positions that have few real quality starters. Normally, this will mean C, 2B, SS and RP. Then get low dollar players (or later round players) from positions that have the most talent (see Appendix B Fantasy Baseball Supply and Demand

Table). The OF tends to have tons of talent. Wins (W) are not chased but stolen bases (SB) and saves (S) are.

Ignore One Category

The owner decides to ignore the stats in one category and instead attempts to dominate the others. By focusing their draft budget or early draft picks on the other categories, he can monopolize them. Wins (W), stolen bases (SB) or saves (S) are the categories most often ignored. In this strategy the team will score only 1 point in the ignored category but hopes to average 10 or more points (3rd place or better) in the remaining nine categories for a total score of 91 or more (9 x 10=90 +1 for the ignored category=91). If wins are ignored this strategy is similar to the All RP Strategy. If saves are ignored RPs will not need drafting. For this strategy to work, owners must not be weak in any other categories except the chosen one.

Ignore Two Categories

The owner decides to ignore the stats in two categories and instead attempts to be first in all the others. By focusing their draft budget or early draft picks on the other categories, he can monopolize them. Wins (W) and saves (S) or home runs (HR) and runs batted in (RBI) are the two categories most often ignored. In this strategy the team will score only 1 point in the ignored categories but hopes to average 11 or more points (2nd place or better) in the remaining eight categories for a total score of 90 or more (8 x 11=88 +2 for the ignored categories=90).

If wins and saves are ignored, SP and RP will not need drafting. The pitching staff can come from middle relievers and set up men, most of whom will go undrafted. If HRs and RBIs are ignored, then owners can focus on batters who steal bases and hit for above average and a quality pitching staff. However, this strategy can be affected by minimum requirements. For example, if 1200 innings (high requirement) are required to be pitched (or else you get last place for ERA and WHIP), then set up men are not the answer.

The main advantage of this theory is the low maintenance required for WDIS and it is easy to draft when two categories are ignored. **For beginners, I recommend using the Ignore Two Categories and skipping HRs and RBIs.**

Balanced Team Theory

Simple, draft or budget your money to finish third or fourth in all of the ten categories. Third place gives 10 points and 4th will give 9 points. So a score of 95, if the balanced team theory is successfully implemented, is expected. This strategy means NOT ignoring any categories. Often it means not bidding/drafting the overvalued big names but instead looking for value in the middle and late rounds with no name players that can support the fantasy team late in the season. This may be the hardest of all the strategies.

LIMA (Low Investment Mound Aces) Strategy

Another term for this is draft hitters early and often and your pitching later. Focus is on two or three quality SPs who can be picked up late. They need to be strikeout pitchers (6 or more per 9 IP) who do not give up too many walks (2:1 K/BB ratio) or HRs (1.0 or less per 9 IP). The last ratios can be combined into a BB+HR/9 IP of 4.0 or less. The idea is to find good pitchers who have yet to blossom and who may not get many wins based on their team run support.

In auction formats, only 23% ($60) out of a $260 budget goes to Pitching (77% - $200 is for hitters). You want to be in the top 1/3 of saves, Ks, ERA and WHIP. You do not worry too much about wins with the LIMA plan; however, you are not completely ignoring it like the Ignore One Category strategy.

One problem with this strategy is that if everyone does it, hitters end up overpriced along with the pitchers who LIMA owners are targeting.

No Player Over $30 Strategy

This is an auction strategy in which you simply never pay more than $30 (11.5% of your $260 budget) for any player. It forces an owner not to reach for over-valued players and instead assemble a solid roster of everyday players at reasonable prices. It is an even better strategy for keeper leagues (see Chapter 14) since you get good players for the future. The key is do not have money left over. If you need a player at a critically manned position, do not hesitate to spend a little over $30 to draft him. The alternative, not having a starting player at that position, is worse.

All RP Strategy

This strategy can only be used in leagues that **do not have high minimum IP requirements**. Owners draft RPs and skip SPs. Any money or draft picks saved by avoiding SPs goes into hitters. The idea is to ignore wins (W) (sound familiar?) and focus on saves, K, ERA and WHIP.

Value Based Drafting

Value-based drafting (VBD) is an advanced theory and specific details are beyond the scope of this book. However, VBD suggests using your overall cheat sheet and **drafting the best players available at any positions for the first 10 rounds or so,** then filling the rest of your roster based on need and some sleeper picks. Unfortunately, this can lead to multiple SPs or RPs at the expense of 1B and 3B unless you fully understand what VBD is based on. Therefore, I do not recommend VBD for beginners.

General Advice

To Close or Not to Close

There are many disagreements on a closer strategy in FB. Some advocate staying away from closers. Matthew Berry of The Talented Mr. Roto, and now ESPN fame, has as his mantra "never pay for saves." Draft RP late and try to add them in free agency when the inevitable RP melt down occurs and some are promoted to be RP in April/May/June. Still others say avoid the top closers and settle for a few midranked closers as they have just as good a chance of 30+ saves as anyone. Then there are the pundits who preach draft dominant closers. The theory is that the top closers are so rare that they are too valuable to pass up. They use few innings yet have great K/IP ratios, low ERAs and WHIP and are the only players who can contribute to the elusive save category. And some of the lower tier RP can harm your ERA and WHIP too. But they can also get you just as many saves.

I spoke of tiering earlier and RP is no different. Expect 4-5 to be elite, 4-5 to be good, 4-5 to be above average but too costly and 4-5 to be great value (just after the middle RP). After these 20 RP will be the 4-5 that are risky (due to age, team, job security, etc.) and then the last six or so that are good spot-fillers.

Most owners in leagues that start 9 pitchers start 3 closers. Some owners draft 3 RPs, others have 2 RPs and a middle reliever or set up man. **I suggest waiting until the 10th round or later for closers.**

Target First 5 Picks

No matter which strategy you use, you can plan on who will be available for your first five picks. Look at who will be available based on your draft spot and determine which players each strategy will give. The first 60 players drafted should be pretty well known. If not, look at an overall cheat sheet from a magazine or your league website. ESPN has ADP (average draft position) on the player's page under research. YAHOO has average pick on the player's page under "Sort By" then "research."

Do not take risks with your first five picks! If the words "question mark" are involved with a player under consideration for drafting in the early rounds - skip him! So avoid injury prone players (this means pitchers by default). **Make the first five players all hitters.**

Easy Draft Plan - Stud at Each Position

For the beginner the best advice is to play it safe. Do not take risks early, wait until the middle to late rounds before you draft risky players like rookies, veterans returning from injury or minor league players with potential. Balance is the key. You need to have good hitters and pitchers so that your start/sit decisions are easy.

The easiest plan is to draft a stud at each of the major positions (1B, 3B, OF, SP and RP). In this case, **you want to get a top 10 player at each of the five player positions with multiple studs**. You are sacrificing strength at other positions in general because you must draft them much later, but you gain by having strength at these positions. Why this plan? It makes your start/sit decisions each day/week much easier if you have a clear player who should start at these positions. It is a no brainer that each will be your starter unless they are hurt or off for the day.

To do this you will need to go into the draft with a plan of drafting a 1B, 3B, OF, SP and RP early. In the first round, get the best hitter available, either a 3B or 1B. Draft a 3B first since there are fewer top 3B around, and then add a 1B in round 2. Follow up with a OF in round 3 and then concentrate on pitching in rounds 4 and 5. This is a little early for pitching but the easy plan is a simple plan. So rounds 1-5 will be:

Round 1   3B or 1B
Round 2   1B or 3B
Round 3   OF
Round 4   SP (Sure thing veteran SP, Top 10)
Round 5   RP (Top 5 RP)

In rounds 6-8 you then draft another OF and a 2B and SS. So, after round 8 you have a 1B, 2B, SS, 3B, 2 x OF and SP and RP. You have all of your starting infield positions filled (except C which you will draft much later). Round 9 will be SP. Later rounds will be OF, C and SP and a RP plus backups.

(See Appendix E - Easy Draft Plan)

Hard Draft Plan – 75 HR/SB First Three Picks

A more difficult draft plan to implement is the "75 HR/SB with first three picks" (See Appendix F Hard Draft Plan). With this plan, you play the numbers and draft hitters early and often. You draft hitters with your first six draft choices. Your first pitcher is drafted in the seventh round. Draft another SP between the 8th and 12th round. Or alternatively draft three SP but not until rounds 9-12. Grab a closer in the 10th round. So draft 7-8 hitters and 2-3 pitchers (at least 1 SP and 1 closer) in the first 10 rounds. Add the rest of your SP and RP in rounds 19th or later. Look for SP with an ERA under 4.0 and a high K/IP ratio and sleepers.

30 hitters hit over 30 HRs in 2009. In 2010, only 17 hit over 30 HRs. In 2009 and 2010, only 17 hitters managed over 30 SB. So, HRs and SBs do not grow on trees. You need to be methodical about who you draft that can provide 75/75 in the first three rounds (your power studs). Do you draft a power hitter and speedster or go for a balanced approach and three players with 25/25 potential? Most power or speed players fall into the 35-40 category for either HRs or SBs. Do you draft a stud HR hitter like Albert Pujols, Joey Votto or Miguel Cabrera (all 1B) or a 50 SB type player like Rajai Davis (OAK, OF)?

Cheat Sheets

Cheat sheets (See Appendix G Cheat Sheets Sample) consist of players ranked from best to worst at each position based on projected fantasy points for the upcoming season. In other words, the projected highest scoring 1B will be ranked first and then the next highest scoring 1B and so on, based on what you think they will do in the season ahead. **Be careful about projections, sometimes the player with the most HRs will not always be ranked #1.** Each position should be ranked with as many players that could be drafted. If possible, look at last year's draft in your league and use that as an estimate of how many 1Bs, 2Bs, etc. will be drafted and make sure you have that many, and a few more, in your rankings. As a minimum, have 30 C, 35 1B, 30 2B, 30 SS, 35

3B, 85 OF, 85 SP and 40 RP ranked on your cheat sheets. **More fantasy teams mean more players drafted.**

Another vital ranking on your cheat sheets needs to be an overall ranking of the top 100-200 players. This serves as a "best of" list and you can use it to draft the best hitter or pitcher when faced with that choice. Be careful though, as overall rankings usually place SPs and RPs too high since they score so many points. However, since both positions have little differences between the 3rd player and the 20th player, wait and draft SP and RP in the late rounds. **Use your overall rankings early in the draft for the best available player (until about round 10 or 11) and then use the positional rankings to fill needs.** For example, "I need a catcher so who is the best one left."

Cheat sheets are like taking your notes into an open book test in school. They help you decide what is right and what is wrong and you want the best information on them. Just as you did when taking those final exams, highlight important information (players you really want: sleepers for example) so that it is easy to see in the heat of the moment. If the cheat sheets are so messy that you cannot understand what the information is, that does not help you. Make sure that your cheat sheets have player's names, MLB team names and especially positions. The team names will prevent you from mistakenly drafting all players from the same MLB team.

If the cheat sheets are not based on your scoring system, then you are comparing apples to oranges when it comes time to draft. **The scoring system used to rank players must be the same as your league scoring rules or very close in order to have good rankings.** How do you get the rankings?

Rankings can be done in many different ways. There is one easy way and that is to use a premium service like *www.rotowire.com.* I discuss them in detail in Chapter 12 - Resources. If you pay for their services, you can get rankings for the draft and each week for starters based on your exact scoring system. The cheat cheats they provide are easy to read and use. Rotowire provides several formats for cheat sheets: you can download a software program that lets you create customizable cheat sheets or simply print out a pre-made cheat sheet from their site based on many of the most common scoring systems around.

Another easy way is to use a pre-printed magazine cheat sheet (or one provided by your league website). However, make sure it is updated prior to your draft. So if you bought a copy of *Fantasy Baseball Index magazine* (see Chapter 12 Resources), you could use their cheat sheets (which are outdated since they came out in Feb.) and simply update them by replacing players who have retired, been injured, promoted/demoted, etc.

The hard way to do rankings is to do them on your own. If you insist on going this route, here is a quick method. Rank each position separately.

1) Start with last year's statistics (based on fantasy points scored, if available) with as many players ranked as you think will go in the draft (see minimums earlier). Your league's website should have this for the previous year.

2) Replace any players who have retired or been suspended for the year. Their replacements may not be as good, or as bad, but this is a good starting point.

3) Look at the number of games played for each player. If less than 146, check to see if they were injured. If so move them up to where they would have been had they played 146 out of 162 games. So if a 1B has 150 FPs and only played 110 of 162 games, assume he will score 200 next year and move him up accordingly.

Expected FPs = (146/# games played) x Fantasy Points from last year

---

Note 146 games used since this is the average for all hitters in MLB.

---

4) Do the reverse for any players currently expected to miss games due to injury or suspension. **For injured players, add an extra week missed simply because they will not be at 100% right away.** So, if a player is expected to miss the first 2 weeks due to an injury, use 3 weeks out.

Expected FPs = (146 - # of games missing/146) x Fantasy Points from last year

Same 1B who we expected to score 200 in a full season is now projected to be 171.

5) Add rookies and other player movements by looking at the team's depth charts. If a rookie is supposed to start right away, then he will knock the old veteran down or out of your ranking. If a team adds another good 1B, that may decrease the existing 1B points.

6) Account for team upgrades/downgrades. If a team improves at RP, bump up the SP wins a bit, if the infielders improve move the SP ERA down and vice versa. A new manager who changes the way the offense is run can also change expected points from players, both positively and negatively.

7) Once your preliminary rankings are done, compare them to others. If any player is very high or very low relatively speaking, re-evaluate.

8) The last step is to use your gut. Look at your rankings and move players up or down a little bit based on what you think will happen this season, based on what you have read, heard or seen.

These steps are a good start for a beginner who wants to create their own rankings. You can do the same technique at each position to find players who are unnoticed but have the potential to breakout. But what about the overall rankings? How do you know whether 1B20 is more valuable or SP25? The overall rankings will tell you this, but it is based on many factors, including how many teams are in the league, the scoring system, the roster size for teams and the starter requirements. For a beginner, I recommend using an overall cheat sheet from a FB magazine based on the same scoring, # of teams, roster size and starting rosters as your FB league. But use it simply to create a blank overall ranking based on position. (i.e. ignore the names on the overall sheet that is perfect for your league, use the ordering of positions.) For example, ranking 1-12 is 1B, SS, 3B, 3B, 2B, OF, OF, 1B, 1B, 1B, 1B and SS and so on until you have 120 positions listed. Now go back and fill in names based on YOUR rankings. So, the first 1B on your 1B rankings goes in the first 1B spot on the overall cheat sheet. The 5th SS on your SS rankings will go in the overall rankings wherever the 5th SS is listed. The idea here is that someone else has figured out the relationships between the 1B20 and SP25 and you use that information combined with who you think is the 20th best 1B and the 25th best SP.

Position Strength and Weakness

There is a huge drop in talent from the studs to the lower tier players at some positions. Positions that have many good or great players are strong positions. In 2010, 1B and SP had depth. If a position is strong (or deep) you can delay drafting that position and still get good value. On the other hand if a position is weak (or shallow), i.e. there are fewer stars there or less good players, like SS, 2B and C; then you need to draft a stud early to avoid a dud starting for you all season. A position can be weak because of a huge drop off in hitting ability after the studs or simply because there are not enough good players to go around (OF and C).

Category Strength and Weakness

The same drop off can be seen in categories as well as positions. SB and HR are the two categories where "category scarcity" comes into play. In 2009, only 17 players stole over 30 bases. Three of those 17 had over 60 stolen bases (Jacoby Ellsbury, BOS, OF; Michael Bourn, HOU, OF and Carl Crawford, TB, OF). In 2010, 17 players had over 30 stolen bases. But only one had over 60 (Juan Pierre, CWS, OF). To say there are a few stud base stealers out there is an understatement. Remember only 30 players hit more then 30 HRs in 2009 and only 17 managed the feat in 2010.

In pitching, it is easy to find pitchers who should win games, but much harder to find pitchers who will win games and have many strikeouts.

Draft players who are good in multiple categories. Simply stealing tons of bases is not enough to win championships. You need to find players that contribute in multiple categories in order to dominate in enough categories to win. Do not overrate one category. At the end of the season, if you lead your closest competitor by one steal you have done well. If you lead by 20, you have overrated that category.

Position Runs

At some point in the draft there will be a run on a position. Normally this is at SP, RP and C. Do not follow the crowd. Just because many RP are drafted ahead of you does not mean you need to draft a RP. Zig when others are zagging and you are more likely to discover player value.

Use Tiers to Draft

Draft from the highest then scarcest tiers first. If you find there is only one 1st tier player left, draft him since he is the highest tier player available. If you find yourself with three 2nd tier 1B and two 2nd tier 2B, draft a 2B since that position is the scarcest (least available) of your two highest tiers. Always try to look ahead to the next round and try to estimate how many players in the tiers will remain. A tier with more players is less likely to be depleted before your next pick.

When it is time to draft backups, focus on backing up your weakest positions first. Positions drafted early in the draft are the strongest and those starting positions drafted last are the weakest. If you drafted Alex Rodriguez (NYY, SS) with your first pick and Geovany Soto (CHI-N, C) with your 18th pick, SS is a strong position and C is your weak position. **Reverse the order of your draft when drafting backups**. SS should be your last pick if SS was your first pick in the draft.

Do not forget the past

If you only focus on last year's statistics you will miss significant recent history that can predict the future better. For example, if a batter missed some of last season due to injury, his HR and RBI totals will be much lower than his average. Only by looking at his three-year average can you determine what this year could bring.

Draft Tips

1) Draft potential over mediocrity (youth over aging middle-of-the-road vet)
2) Draft NL P over AL P
3) Draft COL hitters and not COL pitchers
4) Draft great hitters before great pitchers
5) Draft good hitters before good pitchers
6) Draft a multi position player over a single position player
7) Draft a player at a position that is scarce before a player at a position that is heavy
8) Draft from a higher tier than a lower tier
9) Ratio of hitters to pitchers about 2-1.
10) DH/Util- Be leery of players who are DH only. I.e. cannot play a position

SP

    Pitchers have four basic types of pitches: fastball, changeup (also known as off-speed pitch), and two breaking balls known as the curveball and slider. A pitcher needs a good fastball to setup his other pitches. That is why more fastball pitchers make it to MLB initially and then they adapt by learning more pitches.

    The fastest pitch (a fastball) is around 97 MPH. The slowest pitch (curveball) is 60+ MPH. About 2/3 of pitches in the strike zone are swung at (64.4%), so just getting the ball over the plate does not guarantee success. In many cases, throwing the ball over the plate is exactly what a pitcher does not want to do as a good hitter can drive it for a HR especially if the ball if a little up in the strike zone. Instead, the pitcher, batter and to some extent catcher participate in a game of cat and mouse, baiting each other and trying to gain any advantage.

1) **Good pitchers always pop up throughout the season that were not drafted**
2) **Pitchers have lots of injuries (ligaments, torn rotator cuffs and blisters) so wait on drafting them!**

Materials

What do you need to draft? The first thing is those cheat sheets we just discussed. They are a must. If possible, try and get them so that they are compact. The overall rankings could be on one page and the SP and RP on another page, finishing up with position players on the last page.

If you play in a league with playoffs then another essential piece of information is the MLB schedule for your league's playoffs. A single piece of paper should have those scheduled games on it. Highlight the teams that play the worst teams during the fantasy playoffs weeks. This gives you a quick reference when you are on the draft clock as to which teams have the best matchups those weeks. So far we have 4 pieces of paper: 3 cheat sheets and an MLB final weeks schedule. Consider bringing a ***Fantasy Baseball Index*** magazine (mentioned in Chapter 12 Resources) to hide your cheat sheets from prying eyes and as a crutch in case you lose some of your materials.

Do not even think about bringing a laptop to the draft unless you are proficient enough to work it and draft at the same time. Most of us are not. Do bring several pencils so that you can line through the names of the players on your cheat sheets as they are drafted by other owners. Avoid using pens because, inevitably, some owner will make a mistake and then you cannot erase your mark through that player if you used a pen. **Circle the players that you draft so that you can see their names, teams and positions easily.** Do not mark through your own player's names and positions.

Mock Drafts

Practice, practice, practice…you have heard that drilled into your head since you were a child. Practice does make perfect, especially when dealing with something as fluid as a FB draft. No two drafts are the same. By practicing you will be better prepared for the unexpected. If you have never participated in a draft, simply practicing once will give you a much better appreciation for the tasks ahead. But how do you practice drafting?

Mock drafts are practice drafts. They can occur with other humans as the other owners or with a computer's artificial intelligence (AI) acting as one or more of the owners. If you want to face some human competition, sites like Mock Draft Central www.mockdraftcentral.com offer free and easy mock drafts. ESPN has a great mock draft website too. Some software programs have functions that you can use by yourself to mock draft. In all instances, make sure the rules (scoring, # of teams, roster size, starters, etc.) are as close to your league rules as possible. Don't be afraid. The mock drafts do not count; they are simply a way to practice different strategies or to get a feel for what a draft is like. Thomas Jefferson once said, "I am a great believer in luck, and I find the harder I work, the more I have of it." Obviously, he was not referring to FB, but it applies to mock drafts. The more you do, the better you will be.

How to Have a Good Draft

1) Be prepared. When I say this, I mean have your materials ready, and know who is retired, suspended, in the hospital, in the pokey, and generally collecting an MLB paycheck. Know the rules for starter positions (i.e. do you start one catcher or two, how many OF). ESPN has a health status that says DL 15/60 or DTD. YAHOO says DL and has a red asterisk denoting new player notes.

2) If you have a co-owner, work out who does what in advance, discuss strategy in advance and talk about the players you want, need, and absolutely will not draft. Arm wrestling over whether the team should select a SP or 1B with the first pick on draft day does not a fun afternoon make.

3) Don't lose track of when it is your turn or who else has been picked. Some leagues penalize you when you pick a player already picked. Track who is drafted ahead of you; cross their name off your lists and move on with your life. Get over it.

4) Do not drink and draft. There is a good reason they give out free booze in Las Vegas.

5) Show up on time (early if possible). Nothing starts the league off worse than the 1 p.m. draft starting at 1:45 p.m. If you are going to be late, give good instructions to your most trusted

confidant so that they can draft for you. When you do show up, do not complain about their picks; they are only as good as the guidance you provided.

6) Leave the children at home. They will not enjoy watching you draft, nor will the other owners enjoy babysitting for you while you decide between Randy Wells (P, ChiC) and Phil Hughes (P, NYY).

7) Do not look at other people's draft lists unless they invite you to. Returning from the draft with a black eye only serves to make your spouse suspicious.

8) Do not go to the bathroom right before your pick. See #4 above about no drinking. No fluid, no tinkle.

9) Let the commissioner run things. If he asks you to do your loud attention-gathering whistle, fine. Other than that, it is his show.

Summary

1) Have a Strategy (plan)
    a) Easy – (Appendix E) or
    b) Hard – (Appendix F)
2) Cheat sheets are a must and should be as close to league parameters as possible (# of teams, scoring rules, rosters, etc.)
3) When it is time to draft backups, focus on backing up your weakest positions first.
4) Gather your materials and be ready for the draft.
    a) Cheat Sheets
    b) Sleeper List
    c) MLB schedule
    d) Pencils
5) Participate in mock drafts to get experience.
6) Tier positions to avoid getting caught in runs on positions

Chapter 9 Who should I start?

As the owner of the team, you must set a starting lineup for each day or week, depending on the league rules. You decide which of the players on your team will start (i.e. be the ones to add points to your team) and which will sit on the bench (not add points to your team). The number of starters, and from which position is determined by the rules for your league (see Chapter 4). In many leagues, starters will be 2 C, 1 1B, 1 2B, 1 SS, 1 3B, 5 OF, 7 SP and 2 RP. Some leagues may also have two or three flex players who can be a corner infielder (either 1B or 3B), middle infielder (either 2B or SS), DH or utility player or pitcher with no specific designation (either SP or RP). In the scenario above, with three additional flex players (CI, MI and P), you must name 23 players as starters. Your starting lineup decisions decide the winners and losers in each week's H2H match up. It is the points scored weekly from submitting starting lineups that determines who wins each week and ultimately, which fantasy teams make the playoffs for your league. Even in leagues without a H2H schedule, the results from each daily lineup can be just as pivotal in determining the overall rotisserie winner. In some cases a HR or S on the last day of the season can mean victory.

Many leagues now have their own point projection service that attempts to predict how many points a player will score for the week and, in some stat services, for the next few weeks or remainder of the season. If this is the case, evaluate the system after the first week (since those starters are pretty much your first draft picks) and use it for the entire season. No system is perfect so do not be too hard on the predictor.

Things to look for:

- **How often is it updated (Does it know when a player has been declared out for a game?)**
- **How far off are the predictions from the results (Does it predict too many points or too little points in most cases?)**

- **What does it use to calculate points (Does it use your league rules or is it another scoring system?).**

Quite possibly the best lineup advice is to watch the MLB games (and the pregame shows); especially for the Sunday night and Wednesday night games. If you watch just those two games you are catching the action every few days. Sometimes breaking news is revealed just before the first pitch and can affect your lineup decisions. For example, Player B will miss the game due to an illness or suspension, etc. Perhaps you are starting Player B; now you can bench him and start someone else in his place. You can save yourself some missed FPs by staying on top of the action right before the game starts. Numerous pitcher changes occur over the course of the season. SP#4 for a team cannot go so SP#1 gets an early start on 3 days rest. These are the little things that will not be on most internet sites that are built generically. But some diligence in reading the notes on other sites can uncover these breaking stories. Perhaps your 1B was not going to start again in the hitter friendly confines of COL., today now he will due to a shuffle in his MLB team's lineup. Maybe you will want to rethink your lineup decisions based on that fact.

Fantasy Football Story but …In week 16 of 2009, I had Steven Jackson as a starter. He was listed as questionable (as he had been for the past few weeks), but always played. So I forgot to check his status for the 4 pm game. He did not play in week 16. I found out too late to replace him. It was the difference between finishing 10th out of 228 top competitors in the Fantasy Football Players Championship (www.theFFPC.com) and 16th. It was a huge mistake.

Most information about players comes out 30 minutes prior to game time. Do you need to check every game? No. But a 15 minute review of the players notes once a day should prevent most lineup mistakes like starting a player who hurt himself the night before a day game.

Always look at the statistics from the day before prior to setting your lineup for today. Check to see if any of your players did not have as many plate appearances as one might expect. Remember even in a perfect game, where the pitcher gets 27 outs with no hits or walks, every batter will bat at least 3 times. So a batter should get 3-4 bats as a minimum unless he is pulled early for injury or is walked, since a BB does not count as an at bat. If you see a player with less than three at bats, find out why? The same goes for pitchers. If he was scheduled to start but did not; find out why.

Who Do I Start (WDIS)?

WDIS decisions (also known as start'em or sit'em decisions) are perhaps the hardest choices in the fantasy season. The draft is a one-time event, the consequences of which can be changed with trades or free agent acquisitions (see Chapters 10 and 11). Start/sit decisions are made daily or week after week throughout the season and can drive an owner crazy. Ultimately, the right WDIS decision last week can be the wrong decision this week, or vice versa. The worst situation is where regardless of what you decide, it always turns out to be wrong. Your team's performance suffers when you start the least performing players, and a sense of self doubt creeps in. Sometimes the hardest decision you may have is benching a player and starting someone else. Human behavior makes it easier to stand pat than to make a change. If you have a method for determining who to start, these decisions can be easier. Therefore, you need an easy to follow method to answer the question "who do I start". How about a checklist to follow for start/sit decisions? Is it 100% full proof? No. Is it a great start that will work 80% of the time? Yes. In addition, it is a tool you can use initially until you have some experience playing FB, at which time you can modify the WDIS Checklist to include techniques you have learned.

The order of these steps is important. Later steps should generally not override earlier steps.

Rule #1 – Always set a lineup

I know it sounds simple enough, always set a lineup. However, a typical rookie mistake is not setting a lineup (it can happen to anyone). Set a lineup for each time period even if you are on a cruise ship or on a bus trip. If you know you will be incommunicado (away from the internet), set your lineup early in the week using the best information available. Most websites allow you to set a lineup in advance for every period. That way you gave your fantasy team a fighting chance.

The best plan is to set aside 30 minutes before the first game (from 12:05 PM EST) each day or week to check starters and injury issues for your players and set a lineup based on this information. Most games are at 7:05 pm EST but day games can occur as early as 12:35 pm EST.

Not setting a lineup makes the other owners mad because they may need you to beat your opponent. Do not make that mistake. **Set your lineup for the next day as soon as possible; if nothing else, bench players not playing that day and make substitutions based on injuries.** You can always change it later. Better to have a serviceable lineup in case you get hit by a Guinness beer truck and miss the deadline. This means you need to know your deadline. Some leagues with a weekly lineup state that the lineup has to be in by Sunday night for the week starting Monday, if so do it on Saturday for your initial hack at lineups. Luckily, most leagues use the rule that last week's lineup is automatically used for this coming week until changed. In this case, you will always have a valid lineup, but it may not be the one you want until you actually change it.

Rule #2 – Always begin this WDIS process with your top picks from the draft

This is probably as easy as it is going to get. Start the players you drafted first. Because you drafted them higher, you must think they are better than those drafted later. So in week 1 start the first 1B you drafted. Unless an injury or can't-miss match up occurs in week 1 (see steps below), the first OF drafted goes into OF#1 position, second OF drafted goes into OF#2, and so on.

Rule #3 – Always start your studs

Your studs will be your top five draft picks. Therefore, they will be your every day starters.

If you use the easy drafting plan from Chapter 8, then your studs will be your 1B, 3B, OF, SP and RP. There is a reason why studs were drafted that high. Albert Pujols (1B, STL) and Alex Rodriguez (3B, NYY) should never be benched unless they are hurt and thus on the DL and out for the game (or unless they lose their job; fat chance). **Tip: Any player on a "Can't Cut List" is a stud player.**

A "Can't Cut List" is a list of players so valuable that leagues prevent owners from dropping them (cutting them) because they would provide the gaining owner an overwhelming advantage. Some leagues do not use them because they must be updated for injured players and who determines when an injured player is not valuable any more?

Why? Simple – they are your highest scoring players (that is why you drafted them so high in the first place) and thus they will score the most for you over the season. Do not worry about matchups. They are going to provide you big points if you start them week in and week out. **Start them and forget about them**. Only bench a stud if he is hurt, or suspended. The day you bench one because he is batting against the best SP is the day he hits three HRs and has a career high RBI day. Trying to time their big game is like trying to time the stock market. DON'T DO IT. Consider your studs your index mutual funds and let them ride. If the stud has a slow start or a week or two below average, rest assured that he will return to the mean eventually.

Note: This does not mean he will hit above average the rest of the season to reach his mean.

You just do not want to have him on your bench when he does. If you try to time the big games and the bad games you will be burned more times than not, so start them regardless. You will not lose sleep by starting your studs and them having an off day or two.

Rule #4 – Never start a player who has the day off and don't forget to restart them after their day off.

During the course of the season, MLB gives each team a day off occasionally, called an off day. **Monday and Thursday are the days when some teams have off due to travel.** If your player is not playing on a given day then you will need to replace him as a starter. Off days mean shuffling players from the bench to fill gaps left open as your normal starters are not playing. Just as important is returning an off day player back to the starting lineup once his off day is finished. Some league management systems allow owners to set their lineups for each day individually. Set the next days lineup now, when you replace a player, so that you never find yourself saying, " I forgot to restart my stud player".

Rule #5 –   Do not start doubtful or out players

MLB has what is known as disabled lists (DL) for injured players. Depending on the severity of the injury (and the recovery time) a player is either placed on the 15-day DL or the 60-day DL. If placed on the 60-day DL after august 1, he will be out for the season. A MLB team can call up a replacement player from their minor league system for any player officially on the DL. Another term you may see regarding injured players is day-to-day (DTD). This happens when the medical staff cannot determine when he can play. Diligence on your part in researching the news goes a long way to knowing if you should start a DTD player. What has he done the past few days on DTD status?

Normally, this information will be available on your league website in the form of injury news or with a symbol, letter or note beside the player's name on your team roster page. Pay close attention to these notes as they can give you valuable information concerning the status of a player. Injury reports are fluid lists. Injuries that start off as minor annoyances can change into a rotator cuff injury quickly. Be wary of some of the information. Players are almost always too optimistic about their readiness (usually expressed as a percentage, like "I am at 95% now)

CBS, Fox and ESPN all have a ticker on their pre-game shows that tells the weather and starting lineups (and injury info) for each of the games. **If a player is listed as OUT, bench him immediately and replace him using this checklist.** The same goes for injured players in general. Do this as soon as you find out their status. If you wait, you may forget to do it. Will an injured player play in some cases? YES. However, this checklist is designed to be simple and easy, **so remember if in doubt, bench him**.

Missing a game is different from "not starting a series." Do not overreact to news that your player is not starting. Sometimes coaches will give players a night off. It is the coach's way of keeping his players healthy. Still other times a player may be benched because the coach is trying to shake things up a bit. Don't worry just check his status for the next game and make sure it is not a long term change.

Rule #6 – Ignore Slumps or Hot/Cold Streaks

Players have slumps (bad performances) or hot streaks (good performances). It is a long season (a marathon not a sprint). Over 162 games even your best players will be below average for some time. But research suggests the difference between a slump and a streak can be mainly luck. Of course, an injury is a different matter all together as is developing a skill. We will discuss both of these later. The temptation is to change your lineup, to shake things up when you are near the bottom. In reality, as soon as you bench a "slumping" Matt Kemp he is just as likely to hit 3 HRs and have 5 RBIs.

So how long do you give a player? 2 months or more (depending on where they are in the season) in my opinion because short term statistics are not long enough to evaluate where the player will be by seasons end. This 8-week period does not mean you blindly accept his fate. Instead, look at his mechanics. Is the hitter striking out much more frequently (warning sign)? Is he still making good contact but the balls are just hit directly at someone (leave him in)? Is the SP still striking out batters (good sign)? Or is he giving up more HRs and BB (bad sign)?

Look at how many points your players have scored in the past weeks and use that as a measure of value. Statistical trends will start to break out after the first few weeks (weeks 4-5).

Look for trends, not one-game wonders. Anyone can look special against bad teams. How they scored their FPs is equally important. A good ERA against a bad team from a mediocre pitcher is not what it seems. In this case, he is not performing as well as his statistics indicate. This can fool you into thinking he is better than he really is.

Trends may reveal an injury or a developing skill set. A pitcher who masters a different type of pitch (adding sinker to his repertoire) or a hitter who increases his contact rate (develops more plate discipline) are both examples of a trend that can be exploited rather than a hot streak. Streaks or slumps are fads and cannot be predicted but injuries and skill development can be used to improve your forecasting skills.

Rule #7 – Start multiple position players at the most scarce position

If a player plays1B, 2b and 3B, start him at 2B the minute he is eligible to play 2B. 2B historically is a position known for scarcity in good players. By starting him at 2B you can move another power hitter into the 1B or 3B slot. It is the best use of your team resources.

Rule #8 – Matchups, situational stats and ball parks

This may be one case where rule #3 - Always start your studs is overruled. Usually the team's best SP faces the other teams best SP.

Look for the most favorable match up.

There is one fundamental fact in baseball match up decisions: right-handed batters tend to be more successful against left-handed pitchers and, to an even greater degree, left-handed batters are more successful against right-handed pitchers.

The primary match up focus should be who is pitching to a hitter and where. If your player is facing three of the top pitchers in the league, maybe his backup who is very close in talent, should start if he is facing three middle level pitchers for the week. **For determining a SP match up look at his opponents OPS. OPS is a great measure of a teams hitting ability**

Situational statistics indicate how hitters and pitchers perform in certain situations. For example, at night, on artificial turf, at home, away, with no one on base, with the bases loaded, vs. lefties, vs. righties, etc. One of the best is which specific pitchers a hitter bats best against and vice versa. But be very careful of these. Often the sample size is too small to really be indicative of the correct probabilities. For example, just because a batter is 2 for 20 against John Danks (CHI-A, SP) does not mean that he is likely to hit .100 against him today.

Ball parks get reputations as a pitcher's park or hitter park or as a neutral park. Coors Field, home of the Colorado Rockies, is the strongest hitter's park in MLB. At 5,282 feet above sea level balls go 9% further. Yet due to the dimensions of the fences it does not give up as many HRs as you would think. But the park leads the league in hits and runs.

Chicago's Wrigley Field, home of the Cubs, is known as both a hitter's and a pitcher's park. It depends on the winds. If strong Lake Michigan winds are blowing out, it is a hitter's park and it reverses when they blow in.

Hitter's Parks
1. Coors Field (COL)-most hits and runs but not HRs given up
2. Rangers Ballpark (TEX)-about 5th in all statistics but consistency gets it ranked 2nd overall. ALs most hitter friendly park.
3. Chase Field (ARI)-2nd in hits, runs and doubles/triples but 10th in HRs
4. Great American Ball Park (CIN)-3rd in HRs and Runs
5. Citizens Bank Park (PHI)-some say PHI should be ranked #2

Pitcher's Parks
1. Petco Park (SD)-fewest HRs
2. Busch Stadium (STL)-2nd fewest HRs
3. Safeco Field (SEA)-ALs most pitcher friendly park
4. Oakland-Ala. County Coliseum (OAK)-huge foul territory helps
5. Citi Field (NYM)-opened in 2009 but is working its way up

Do you bench your best hitters because they are batting in Petco Park? No. Do you bench a questionable OF and replace him with a close substitute that is batting in Coors Field? Absolutely!

Some pitchers pitch better away than at home (rare but it does happen). Most batters do better against a certain handed pitcher (lefties or righties).

Another important situation to look for in matchups is the double header. **If a hitter can get the chance to play in two games start him.** That is twice as many chances at runs, RBIs, HRs and stolen bases. If your league has a maximum games limit for positions-think twice about using a player in a double header. They are more likely to be replaced or even benched for the second game and you may get a wasted game start.

Rule #9 – Know Which Pitchers Get 2 Starts in the Week Ahead

This is more for H2H leagues with weekly not daily lineups. Know which of your pitchers will start twice in the week and who his opponents will be for those games. The same can be said for FA pickups. Two pitching starts affords the opportunity for twice as many W, S and K. However, if your league uses an innings pitched (IP) limit you need to be more careful about the quality of the starts you get from each pitcher. As an example, Ivan Hernandez is a known innings eater and you may not want this notoriously low K pitcher using so many of your precious IP.

Rule #10 – Go With the Crowd

Most leagues have a "% owned" or "% starting" statistic included on your team page. If in doubt, use whichever player has the highest owned or starting percentage. In essence you are allowing the collective knowledge of everyone playing FB on that web service to tell you who they are starting. Think of it as phoning a friend for advice.

Rule # 11 – Category Management

If you are trying to gain ground on a specific category (for example saves or steals), then you need to start players most likely to get those category statistics for your team. Starting a SP over a RP or set up man will NOT get you saves. Just as starting a power hitter with no speed will not get you steals. Look at the expected production of a player (most league websites have these projections) and use that to guide the best players for category management.

In the case of category management of SB, the opponent is a big factor. Some pitchers/catchers/teams are good at controlling the running game while others are not so good.

Tiebreakers for Toss-Ups

Use the following only if you have used other methods to determine who to start and you have two or three players who are all about the same and you do not know who to start. The first discriminator is home field advantage. If they are all equal, the players at home should have a little advantage (about 10%). He has had better sleep, has not had to travel and is playing in front of his hometown crowd and knows the stadium better than anyone.

If both are at home, neither are, or that was what made them a toss-up to begin with, then go with whichever will be playing on a nationally televised game. Why? Because now they get to showcase themselves to the nation. Most players feel a little extra excitement about playing on national TV and this should give them a slight edge over other players. They will be bringing their "A" game for the Monday or Wednesday, Saturday, or Sunday night viewing audience. If that is not a factor, use the player you will be able to watch on TV where you live. Obviously, this does not help that player play any better, but at least you can get the satisfaction of watching him perform.

This again is not some magical formula for providing the maximum fantasy points; it is merely a preferred method for extending the joy of fantasy baseball.

Checklist for Toss-Up Starter Decisions
      1) Go with home team players first
      2) Choose those playing in national TV game
      3) Choose a player playing in a game you can watch

Summary
1. See Appendix H for WDIS Checklist.
2. Watch the pregame shows - most information on player status comes out 30 minutes before game time.
3. The checklist for tiebreakers is more for fun, less about FPs.

Chapter 10 How Do I Improve My Team Through Free Agency?

A typical rookie mistake is not making any moves after the draft. Even if you have a successful draft, your work is not over. At some point in the season, you will have a team need. Maybe one RP is removed as the closer and the other is hurt. In that case, you need a RP or two for sometime.

There are three ways to fill a need: from your bench, free agency or through a trade (approach a need in that order). The easiest way to meet a need is through your own bench. If that is not possible, then free agency may be an option. The best (most successful) owners try to improve their team, or at best, block their opponent from improving their team via free agency. For every owner that drafts a great team, another has a weak draft but makes some great in-season additions to make the playoffs.

We all make mistakes at the draft. We may be able to fix these mistakes through free agency upgrades and trades. Free agency is easier than trading because free agency does not involve another owner, but the free agent pool sometimes does not have the talent you need. In those cases, a trade may be your only option (See Chapter 11 – Trades).

Things happen that force you to make changes. Many owners will not conduct any transactions early in the year because they still have faith in their drafted team. This is a good strategy as it takes 6-8 weeks for trends to develop. It is better to wait a few weeks than to be hasty with dropping key players on a slump. An **easy beginner step is to wait until June before making major moves that impact your starters**. Still other owners will rarely make changes unless forced to by injuries.

Look at the statistical leaders each week and see if any were undrafted. If available, look at them more closely. Are they getting the starts only because the star is hurt but will be back soon, are they coming in and replacing the star because of his nagging injuries, or is it a platoon situation and the star is losing the battle? By observing the box score/stat leader boards and doing some research, you can beat other owners to the punch on these up-and-coming players. **Remember: never accept the status quo; always try to improve your team.** At the same time, you need to be careful not to drop your up-and-coming players for the "flavor of the week" (i.e. players who have done very well in the latest week of competition but have not shown other indications of greatness).

Improving your team

Every 2-3 weeks check your league standings in detail. Look at each category and where you stand in relation to other teams within each category. If you are leading a category by a large margin, you can ease off on that statistic and start players who are more likely to accumulate statistics in other much needed categories. For example, if you lead saves by 10 with only 1-2 weeks to go, bench your closers in favor of SPs who can get more wins. Alternatively, trade a closer to another team for a power hitter. **Leading a category by more than one unit is a waste at the end of the season**. Better to aim for second place and overachieve than aim for dominance and over achieve.

Formats

All players not on a roster at any given time are either on the free agency (FA) list or on the waiver wire. The waiver wire is for players recently dropped and awaiting processing onto the FA list. Usually a player must stay on waivers for a certain amount of time (2-3 days); during which if another owner requests him and wins (has a higher priority or bids the most FAAB), he can be claimed at the end of the waiver period. Any player not claimed off waivers will go to the FA list. The FA listing includes players who are free (hence the name) to be picked up by the first owner who requests them. Another format requires that all players be claimed off waivers, so none are readily available. Some leagues use the FA list and waiver wire as the same vehicle. These leagues use a waiver wire priority to determine who can claim a player.

Free Agency Upgrade

Free Agent Types

There are two types of players to pick up in free agency. Those who will be used just for one week (or few days) to fill an injury need or suspension gap and those that will be added as a permanent member of your fantasy team. So, there are short-term adds and long-term adds. **The short-term free agents (STFA) can be picked using the methods in Chapter 9-Who Do I Start.** He will only be used for that one week so choose who is the best available player at that position and add him. Do not fall in love with him as he will be axed (dropped) the next week, once your injured or suspended player returns to action. Do not forget to look at what the actual teams are doing when you think STFA. If a team is winning often that means it has some players who are doing well too and they may be just what you need as a short term fix.

Long-term free agents (LTFA) are another matter. LTFAs will be on your team until they are hurt, benched or replaced by another LTFA. Therefore, there needs to be much more planning in the decision to add them. Consider their injury history, the team they are playing for, the upcoming schedule, etc. **Use the rankings checklist in Chapter 6 for choosing LTFAs.**

There are three types of LTFAs. Starters, backups for the injured and sleepers or hunch players that you cannot afford to let sit on the waiver wire. Before grabbing a player from the waiver wire, ask yourself: why am I doing it? Why do I think he will perform now?

1) Look at past performance. If he failed to produce as a starter earlier and is playing only because the starter is injured, that does not necessarily make him a good starter.

2) Be conscious of opportunity; make sure he is going to play. There is no reason to pick up a position player who steps in for one week (while the starter is out) and has a career week, if that backup will never see the field again all season because the main starter is so good. Even if the NYY backup 3B plays a great game and does well, do you really think Alex Rodriguez (NYY, 3B) is going to be benched? No, opportunity is critical. Moreover,

opportunity comes from the benching of the starter, a return from injury, or a trade. Injuries to the starter also create opportunities but those are a little harder to predict. To realize the potential opportunities you need to do long-term thinking, not short-term planning. He is a low risk/high reward player, so add him one week earlier than other owners. He is an expensive risk the next week. Do not forget contractual issues. If a team has drafted or traded for a player high enough, they will want to see him on the field.

3) Supporting players are an integral part of a player's game. SPs need good RPs to get wins; RPs need good SPs to give them save opportunities, both types of pitchers need a good infield to catch the ball and turn the double plays; hitters need less than outstanding pitchers throwing to them.

4) Look for players dropped by other owners too early. Is the player in a slump, but is consistent year in and year out? Regression to the mean will dictate that he should put up better numbers the rest of the season. Is it a SP who just faced three of the top 10 hitting teams? If so, grab him. One owner's trash is another owner's treasure. **If time limited, look at who the top teams have dropped; as a beginner the top teams cast offs may be better than who you have drafted.**

5) Get players who will benefit your team. If you have three stud RPs and another falls in your lap, ask yourself if there is another player at another position that you need more. Perhaps you should get the stud RP and trade another one of your star RPs to get a better player at another position.

Minor League Prospects

Each of the MLB teams has a minor league farm system to cultivate players. These minor league teams are placed in a three-tier league system called A , AA (pronounced double A) and AAA (pronounced triple A). Players almost ready for the major leagues are on the AAA teams. Lynchburg, Virginia, where I grew up, has a team in the Carolina League (A) called the Lynchburg Hillcats now affiliated with the Cincinnati Reds. I have fond memories of watching Darryl Strawberry, Dwight Gooden and Lenny Dykstra play there. Of course, back then the team was associated with the NY Mets.

In reality, if the FB league is competitive, by the time a prospect is called up to the big leagues, another owner has already added him to his lineup. You have to look ahead for these players. Look at AAA and AA players with great stats (great players facing inferior competition should shine). **Players under 25 and playing for desperate organizations have the best shot of promotion to MLB.** The younger an impressive player is the more chance of promotion and potential.

Actions in the Preseason

Look at the position battles (especially C/1B/SP/RP) at training camp. If a rookie has a chance to beat out a veteran at a skill position, grab the rookie (if available) BEFORE he is named a starter. In other words, be proactive and grab the player before he wins the job. At worst, you can drop him after week 8 when he does not start. At best you have gazumped (bamboozled) all the other owners and made a big splash in the FA market before the season starts. **Rookie OFs have the best chance to succeed of any rookies, if given the opportunity.**

Watch for injuries and be ready to grab their replacement, even if only for a short time. This gives you potential trade bait for the other owner whose player is hurt. Do not forget to remind him that his player is hurt now and may have problems all year with the nagging injury, so he needs his backup. It also blocks that owner from replacing his injured player with that backup.

Actions in the first half of the Season

Do not do anything for a few weeks unless forced to by significant injuries, player suspensions, retirement, etc. Some players will start slow. There is no reason to drop a 3rd round draft pick simply because he puts up a few goose eggs (zero points) against tough pitchers. **If you drafted someone in the early or middle rounds, you should hold onto them and let them have time to develop.** Do not overreact in the first two months. FB is a marathon, not a sprint. Do not be the owner who says, "DOH! I wish I had just stayed calm and not cut my 1B too early." June means call ups from the minor league; now you can start to evaluate your team.

Do not expect much change in MLB starters the first month of the season. Just as you should not bench your studs too hastily, coaches who have named starters want to give them a chance too. Build a watch list (list of potential players for your team at each position that are available on the FA list) the first few weeks of the season and be ready to go after the first month.

Consider upgrading your pitching staff (SPs especially) if yours is not performing by May. SP are a dime a dozen and some will be in the Top 60 that were not drafted.

By June, be ready to cut some of your late round picks that are not panning out.

Actions after Midseason (after the All Star Break)

Look for rookies with pedigree (did well in college) who are expected to be called up from the minor leagues (especially those behind an aging vet). The "win now" mentality of MLB means rookies are more likely to get a shot on MLB teams out of the playoff hunt who are trying to develop new talent for the future. Look to teams who are 15 games behind (too far out of the playoff hunt) by August. Now look at their schedule for Aug and Sept. What will their record be then? Those weak teams will experiment with their starting rosters.

Many leagues stop transactions (trades/waiver wire pickups and add/drops) once the fantasy playoffs begin or even a few weeks before the fantasy playoffs begin. If this is the case, you need to make some team adjustments before the deadline. If you ran with only one player at a position during the year (rotating and adding/dropping based on matchups/injuries) then you now need to get a starter to stick with and a backup in case the starter gets hurt. Also, get rid of any players you do not absolutely need as either insurance or starters, and add SP and power hitting depth. In some years, nearly 50% of the SPs in week 22 may not be the ones from week 1. Why? Injuries, suspensions, trades, rest for playoffs, benching, coach's decision, etc. So, before the deadline, go with a starting roster and an extra MI, CI, OF, SP and RP if able. This will leave some room for more rookie sleepers.

Think about playoff matchups when evaluating FA pickups. Who will he face in weeks 22-26? Use this as a discriminator.

Free Agency Blocking Strategy

Blocking – This is a tactic in which you grab a free agent player your opponent needs even though you do not need him. A perfect example occurs when a player goes down with an injury. The RP hurts his hand and is placed on the 15 day DL. Your opponent this week is the owner of that player. If the new short term RP fill-in is on the free agent list, then you would be wise to add him.

This is beneficial to you in many ways. First, the backup may prove to be a good RP to start this week based on his matchups or your RP status. Secondly, the starter may be out for the rest of the season, in which case you just picked up another starting RP. Perhaps best of all, you have BLOCKED this week's opponent from picking up a serviceable RP. He will be cursing you when he sees that you have scooped up his backup even though you do not need him. This can prove to be a very successful strategy.

The same thing can happen even if you do not want the backup. Say, for example, that Heath Bell (SD, RP) is injured for your opponent this week; perhaps Mike Adams (SD, RP) does not appeal to you as a good closer to have regardless of the status of Heath Bell. In that case, you can still BLOCK your opponent by grabbing the best RP available on the free agent list. This prevents your opponent from getting the better backup, assuming he does not have a suitable backup on his bench. RP, 2B, SS and C will usually be the positions for which this strategy works best. Other positions (SP and OF) are too deep.

Not only can you "block" an opponent you face for the week but you can also block all of the other owners too. Even if that popup contributing player is not starting for your team, having him means that he is not starting on someone else's team.

13 Free Agent Tips

1) Always have a "watch list" of at least two players from each position that you would add if you had an injury. Use your rankings - adjusted for injuries, suspensions and opportunities. Think about it this way: "If I could keep two more players at each

position, who would I draft?" Perhaps they are sleepers that you want to pick up if they start to perform. Keep up with who is available and who was just released. When another fantasy owner adds a player, check out who they dropped and evaluate them for potential. Many times these are players drafted who have just not performed lately. Add them to your team if there is a reason to expect a rebound or if they are better than the players that you have on your team. **The players that are dropped most often, when a good FA or waiver wire player becomes available, are OF and SP. Always be on the lookout to add one of these if they can help you.**

NOTE: Many websites will let you mark players as watch list; this makes it easy to monitor them as the season progresses and allows you to delete players that others have added.

2) Use the upcoming schedule for LTFAs. Do they have favorable matchups? If a SP, look for weak hitting teams or pitcher-friendly ball parks on their schedule ahead. If position players, look for weak pitching teams or hitter-friendly ball parks.

3) **Lead, don't follow, in free agent transactions; plan for your additions at least two weeks in advance.** Try to be one-step ahead of the other owners. They will be thinking one week ahead. If you are looking for a SP that has a good match up in two weeks, you are much more likely to get him than if you wait until one week away and have to compete with every other owner who is also looking for a replacement player for that position. **Don't forget minor league players who may be called up. Jump on these up-and-coming players before other owners.**

4) **Do not waste roster spots on an extra C, RP or 2B/SS unless the rules force you to do so.** If the rules state that you must carry a certain number of those positions (such as two each) then you have no choice. If the rules do not state how many of each position you must have on your roster, carry only the starters and no backups for C, RP and SS/2B. Why carry no backups from each position? It frees up roster spots for sleeper

picks in other, more critical, positions. Simply carrying the starters at all three positions will free up three places for sleepers.

5) Grab the backup RP if the primary RP starts to have minor injuries or if the head coach indicates a change may be forthcoming. Definitely grab the backup (called handcuffing) if your starter begins to come up a little lame at times. Nagging little injuries late in the game can be an indicator of problems ahead. The head coach making statements like "Trevor Hoffman (MIL, RP) is our man for now," may be an indication of things to change in the future. Read between the lines.

6) If looking for a short term (1-2 week) pickup, make sure he has a great match up in the week you are going to use him. For example, Chase Utley (PHI, 2B) is your 2B. Chase is out for one week due to soreness in his throwing arm. So you need to add a 2B for week 16. Look to see how many games the replacement will play, where he will bat and who he will bat against (opposing starting pitchers). If looking for a SP fill in, look at how many starts they will get (1 or 2 that week), what kind of ballpark they will pitch in and what is the opposing teams batting average/OPS?

7) A starter's injury can be your ticket to the acquisition of a great player. Look for injuries and grab the backup to the injured player, especially if it is a starting C or RP. What about an injury to your player? Your preparedness will determine the champions from the pretenders. Do you have a backup RP#3 to fill in? Can you trade away some bench depth to recover? If you do not have the new closer, grab him immediately if your starter is out. Some will hesitate and begin to over-analyze. "What if he does not start?" "What if he is not any good?" GRAB HIM NOW. If you wait, someone else will grab him to block you. He will definitely do better than your injured player who is out. **If he does not start, then try to grab the person who did start or make other plans for next week. Having a plan (grab his backup) is better than no plan at all.**

Do not forget to look at the FA list for star players who are injured and are off the radar screen. Always keep in mind when they are scheduled to return. You may have to add them a week earlier to keep the other owners out. Remember to be cautious with them when returning from injuries, but many times a pickup in week 20 or 21 can turn into a jewel at playoff time.

Another player to watch for is the one who was sent to the minor leagues for rehabilitation. Keep an eye on them especially if they have shown good stuff previously.

8) Avoid one-week wonders. Some owners will add a OF or SP who has one great game (ex. 3 HRs or 8 scoreless innings). Evaluate him but also look critically at his performance. Was he a first week wonder? Did he play because the star was injured and could not play? Is he a new player on the team and this was just the beginning? Is he a hitter who had three RBIs off a position player who was pitching to save the bullpen in an extra inning game? A wait and see attitude is better than dropping good players chasing long shots.

9) Analyze game history. You can usually use websites to sort players based on their stats. Look at FP scored, and then look at critical statistics-OBP and SLG. Look at quality starts for a SP. What about their K:BB ratio? A SP with a low ERA but few wins may be losing due to poor run support; more runs from his team could mean more wins down the road. Someone with a good SLG may be just around the corner from more hits and runs. Rookies who are getting more and more at-bats should be considered sleeper material. **The longer you go into the season, the more you will need to look at game-by-game performances**. As an example, it is week 20 and you are looking at a SP to replace an injured SP. A SP with twelve wins, but most of them before the All-Star break, is not as good as a SP with only eight wins, but seven of those are from the last eight games. What have you done for me lately?

10) Look at your minimum and maximum game/inning requirements. There is no reason to add a C or RP if that position is close to maximizing the requirement. Know how close you are to these requirements and judge the time until the end of FA.

11) Carry an extra RP for when the FA period has ended. Get your spare RP before the end of the free agency period, if there is an end. This makes sure you are covered in case of injury after the FA period ends. There is nothing worse than seeing your RP sidelined for the next 2-3 weeks and your playoff-bound team becoming closer-less.

12) Always check the league's transactions daily.

13) The MLB trade deadline is 31 July. Pay close attention to trades. Sometimes a good player goes to a great team and becomes even better. Other times a good player goes to a bad team and flounders. Know the MLB trade deadline and watch for opportunities.

Free Agent Acquisition Budget (FAAB) Notes

FB is different than FF in that you have almost twice the weeks in FB (26 vs. 16). Assuming you start with a $1,000 FAAB, expect to pay anywhere from $50-$200 for a week 1 new starter; $150-$350 is the typical range for a good pickup during the season. Rarely do owners spend over $400 on any one player (too much of the budget spent on one player). Most of the spending occurs in weeks 1-2 and 6-10 and then it decreases as the weeks go by until the last week before the transaction deadline, where it picks up, presumably because owners know that they can spend all their money then. There is no reason to save money. You may see up to $900 later in the season if a new starter emerges (that is a sure thing) due to a season-ending injury. That, of course, assumes the owner has that much FAAB left.

Summary

1) Do not assume your team is perfect after the draft. Look for weaknesses (injuries, weak players, too many at one position, etc.) and players available after the draft who can fix the weaknesses.

2) Why use free agency? To fill a need for an injured, suspended, demoted, or poor performing player that cannot be met through your own bench.

3) Look for opportunity in the form of injury, suspension or trade of a starter.

4) Rookie OFs have the best chance of any rookies for success.

5) Do not drop early or mid-round draft picks too early in the season unless they are out for the season.

6) SP and OF are the easiest to upgrade through free agency.

7) Have two catchers and closers before the FA period ends.

8) Use the same rules for WDIS decisions when trying to find a short-term (one-week) replacement. Use the checklist for ranking players when looking for long-term free agents.

Chapter 11 How Do I Improve My Team through Trades?

You can control three of four things that win championships; your draft, your lineup decisions and your waiver wire/free agent transactions. All of these are fully within your control. The other aspect to winning, which you do not control completely, is trades. It involves another human being. That other person is what makes it so tricky. Some owners love to trade, some are afraid to trade and some tolerate it as a necessary evil to improve one's team. Many owners fear trades because they are afraid of losing. If the trade backfires, things could be worse than they were before.

Most owners will come out of the draft thinking they have had a good draft and a perfect team. There is little to be gained by trading then, unless a team has obvious flaws, such as only one RP. Even then the owner may want some time to see how things develop. Trades usually happen after week 5 and not before. Why? It takes a few weeks of frustrating performance before some owners give up the ship. Hardly anyone gives up on a player after week 1. If they do, let me know, I want to play in that league. Injuries can be another reason for trades and they tend to start to pile up after a few weeks. A dip in trades may occur just before the trading deadline because some owners give up on getting a deal done close to a deadline.

Trading is allowed in some leagues, while in others, it is forbidden. The high stakes leagues usually prohibit trades in order to eliminate the possibility of collusion. Collusion is a conspiracy between two or more owners where they intentionally try to improve one team at the expense of another. This is illegal and ruins the fun and joy of playing FB. **I recommend playing in leagues that do not allow trades to prevent any chance of collusion.**

In lesser stakes leagues ($100 or less), trading may be allowed. If allowed, trading can be a fun and interactive way of playing the game. Some say that trading spices things up. One thing is for sure, more arguments come from trades than any other issue.

Trades that are unfair or bad (or perceived to be) can create bad feelings among the owners and toward the commissioner. They can cause teams to quit trying or drop out of the league altogether. **Avoid leagues that allow trades.** Trades are a hassle and a beginner has more chance of getting swindled.

There is an old saying in fantasy baseball, "Better no trade, than a bad trade." Make sure any trade you make benefits your team. Do not accept a trade just to be trading. You can go the entire season without trading. You can offer, counter-offer, accept or reject trades. No one is forcing you to do any of these. No reply after a certain time should be a rejection of a trade. Nevertheless, be respectful and reply to all trade offers. You do not have to accept a trade.

So why trade? Because the chances are high that at some point in the season your team will be affected by injuries, MLB manager start/bench decisions, other players playing better or your players playing poorly. All of these can lead your team to be deficient in one area or another. The need to make a playoff push may nudge a trade here and there too.

Trades can be good, bad, or unfair. Ultimately, you are the one who pulls the trigger on the trade. **If you have to ask if you won or lost, you probably lost because you do not know why you made the trade; make trades that benefit your team.** You need to know how and why they will benefit you. **There are two reasons to trade: build depth (ex. get a better OF in case of injury) or to improve a starter (ex. RP#1 is now much better).**

Trades are more likely to occur in leagues with large rosters and less likely to happen in leagues with smaller roster sizes. Leagues with smaller rosters have more players available via free agency. Many times in a league with a small roster size, the other owner will want a little something extra to get the deal done. With a smaller pool of players on your team, it is hard to create something as a little extra. Often the only way to get the trade done is to give too much. Therefore, it is either a deal that is costly or no deal at all. In leagues with large rosters (typically dynasty leagues), owners have future draft picks, young up-and-coming stars and rookies with potential, all of which can help make a deal. **The more options you have to offer, the easier it is to get a trade done.**

Trading is a game of give and take. Think of trading like being a used car salesperson. You do not want to tell the other person exactly why you want to trade (or what the car's condition really is) because that may scare him away. On the other hand, you need to be as honest as possible so that he does business with you again or at least does not tarnish your reputation with other owners (customers). Good SPs and CIs will always be a desired trading commodity simply because of the law of supply and demand. You will rarely have problems getting takers for a trade involving a CI. The key is to make it worth it for you and the other owner.

Some terms before we proceed:

Proposed Trade – a trade that has been offered to another owner for acceptance. The owner considering it can accept, reject or counter-offer.

Accepted Trade – a trade that has been agreed to by two or more owners and that has been put to the league for approval.

Approved trade – a trade that has been approved by the league as official. Usually approval is given by the commissioner, a vote by owners or by no protest from a set amount of owners.

Types of Trades

1) Players at same position – You trade a SP to Team A and he trades you a SP back. Hopefully both players are of similar value. Then why trade? Maybe one owner likes the other SP better because he is on his favorite team or comes from his alma mater. Perhaps one has a weak playoff schedule or a strong remaining schedule, etc.

2) Multiple player deal – this involves trading multiple players from each team. Usually it will involve one big player from each team. In other words, the player you have to move off your roster anyway, to make room for the main player, can be packaged as part of the trade. For example, you want to upgrade at 2B and you have lots of OF depth. You offer Rajai Davis (OAK, OF) for Ty Wigginton (BAL, 2B). You also offer to give Team A your 2B, Mike Aviles (KC, 2B), for one of his OFs, (NYY, Nick Swisher), who looks promising. You get two players, a 2B and OF and he gets two players, a 2B and OF. You both improve your teams by filling needs.

Trade Partners

There are five types of traders:

    1) The ones looking to swindle

    2) Those looking to trade only if they get the clear upper hand in some way. For example, owners trying to get rid of someone whom they are going to drop in 2-3 weeks anyway; in many cases they are rarely willing to give away good for good.

    3) Those who like to talk trades but never go through with them.

    4) Suckers – those who will accept any trade

    5) Those looking to give and get fairly

    Get to know the other owners' tendencies in your league. Give them what they want, not necessarily what is good for them.

    Focus on owners who want to trade. Do not waste your time or energy with owners who have anti-trading tendencies as noted above. **Anytime you find teams with two good players but who can only start one you have a possible trading partner.**

Steps to Execute a Trade

    1) Identify what you need (your weaknesses). You are weak at 3B. You have two of the league's worst and every time you add/drop one, he turns into a stinker too.

    2) Identify what you have to offer (your strengths). Your team's strength may lie in the fact that you have six power OFs and can only start five per week. You have an extra starting OF to trade.

    3) Look for what you need from other owners' teams. Determine which players in the league, on other teams, will fix your weakness. Have the names ready. You must have some objective in order to know when to proceed. Do not have just one name. "I must have David Wright (NYM, 3B)," is not a need but a want. "I need a top three 3B" is a much better objective.

    4) Determine what the other owner needs.

    5) Make an offer, utilizing your own personal strengths and weaknesses in the trade.

Trade Dos (Steps to a successful trade)

1) Compromise or overcome objections when they do not hurt your team. Sometimes a OF or SP can sweeten the deal enough to get it approved. However, avoid too much compromise. Do not be so wrapped up in getting a trade done that you lose sight of the objective. **Compromising too much just to get a trade done is the worst thing you can do.**

2) Try to make the trade look like the other owner's idea. If you can get him to suggest the trade, you have a higher chance of getting the deal done.

3) State the obvious. Imply everything else. Minimize talking about why a trade is needed. In trades, less talk is more if you can get the other owner to jump to conclusions.

4) Use the "us versus them" mentality to build allies. This is especially helpful in leagues with divisions or where one team has dominated for several years. Try to build up a rapport with other teams in the other division that are fighting a "bully" or dominating team. When trading with an owner from another division, a simple "You need this to beat Team A this year. Do it and I will see you in the playoffs," can work miracles.

5) **Avoid trading with division rivals that can beat you for a title or playoff spot.** Trading with them after you have played them and have a comfortable lead over them is acceptable, especially if they have yet to play your division rival. In that case, the words of the ancient proverb, "The enemy of my enemy is my friend", would apply.

Trade Don'ts (Steps to an unsuccessful trade)

1) Don't congratulate the other owner on the trade. This will naturally make him suspicious of why you are so smug at making the trade.

2) Don't gloat or rub a trade in the face of anyone.

3) Don't get personal or emotional. Never attack an owner's intelligence, personality or family. If you have to walk away, then do so; but do it with dignity. Always say, "Thanks for the offer but I am going to decline. Maybe we can come to something next time."

4) Do not make a trade offer without looking at the other owner's roster. You look foolish offering to trade a RP to a team that has RP as their strength.

5) Never try to trade an injured or demoted player. If you want to move him, let the other owner know the player's situation; doing this one time will ruin any reputation you had as a fair trader.

6) Do not lie or make up stats or quotes. This will lead to other owners finding out and quickly labeling you as untrustworthy. However, if you state that Dan Haren (AZ, SP) is on track to score 20 wins, after he has scored 10 by the All Star break ; that is a valid tactic. The fact that Haren has played an easy schedule in the first half of the season and received 6.1 runs per game in support is something the other owner should evaluate. Statistics do not lie; other's interpretations of statistics is where the lying comes in. Remember Mark Twain – "There are lies, damned lies and statistics."

7) Do not assume that your trading partners rank players the same as you. If you think Joe Mauer (MIN, C) is worth more than Joey Votto (CIN, 1B), try to get a straight up trade. Do not sweeten the deal until asked. **Always start with your lowest (though not insulting) offer.**

Trade Communication

Communication is the key for any successful trade. Always keep the lines of communication open. Start with an innocent "What would it take to get Matt Kemp (LA, OF)?" Even if the other owner says, "Nothing on your team," now you have established some communications and can go from there. **Always ask the selling price first, it may surprise you at how low it really is.** If you start with an offer, you may pay too much. Start out by asking "How much?"

Responses to Trade Offers

Always respond to offers in a timely manner. Nothing turns off an owner more quickly than no response to a trade offer. I hate having my offers just hanging in the wind while the rest of the league moves rapidly forward. If you only check the website twice a week, tell everyone. If you are going on vacation for a week, tell everyone so they will know you cannot communicate in a timely manner.

Some owners start low and like the art of haggling. Anyone who has been to the markets and bazaars of many European or Middle Eastern countries can relate to this tactic. They expect you to bargain and hope you will accept less than they are willing to part with. Counter their lopsided offer with your own reasonable offer (but not your best offer or that will remove some of your own wiggle room). Play their game but with less movement of positions. An offer of trade (even a bad one) is better than no offer at all. At the very least, you get to see who the other owner likes or values on your team and you have opened up some communications with them.

If the trade is totally unacceptable, explain why and move on. Nevertheless, be diplomatic in your explanation why a trade is not right for your team. **Trades are like some people's babies, owners and parents take great offense when their "children" are put in a bad light**. My worst reply is "Would you accept this trade if you were in my shoes?"

Seven Rules of Trading

1) Select trading partners based on need and personality. Look at all the rosters in your league and identify who is strongest where your need is. Now look at those teams and determine where their needs are. A great trading partner is strong where you are weak and weak where you are strong. It is a match made in heaven. You can help him and, for this, he will help you. Do not forget personality either. Remember the trading types. Never give up on any one owner but also do not waste too much time or energy on an owner that obviously does not or will not trade. **Many times new owners (beginners) will make friends with a few owners, develop close ties to them, and subsequently trade exclusively with them**. This is natural; people we know and trust are more likely to become trading partners. Just do not eliminate the other owners simply because you do not know them as well. Always have the trading door open.

2) Criticize in private, praise in public. My dad always told me that and it applies to the players on your team too. Never communicate your displeasure with a player openly. That just allows other owners to know how you feel and gives them the chance to lowball you during future trade negotiations about that player. If you have any criticisms, keep it private. Do not talk bad about your own players. On the other hand, always pump up and promote your players. Use stats to brag about them or use other's "expert" commentary. Other owners will soon covet your players and trade offers will come flooding in when others realize what great players you have.

3) Always do your homework. How will this trade affect my team? How will it affect the other owners team? What does his remaining Strength of Schedule (SOS) look like? What is his fantasy playoff schedule? What is the MLB player's team doing? What is the status of his injuries or his teammate's injuries? Is there any competition for his job?

4) Know your deal breaker. You will not trade these players. Better to know these upfront and maybe even announce them to the other owner as "off the table." No reason to waste time with offers for them.

5) Present your case. If the trade really is win-win, you may have to sell his "win" portion. This could be because he does not see that he has a weakness at a certain position. Point out this flaw to him (diplomatically, of course) so that he can identify his needs.

6) Once the trade is a done deal; forget it ever happened and move on. No reason to gloat that you got a great deal. No reason to treat that owner more favorably in the future just because you got a trade accomplished with him. Do not rue the fact that you did not get everything you wanted. Now focus back on your team and continue to seek out strengths and weaknesses.

7) Establish relationships. Get to know ALL of the other owners. Ask them questions about their lives, philosophies and successes. Once you know the other owners, you can begin to get a better feel on how to handle trade negotiations with them.

Evaluating Trades

The best evaluation is to ask yourself: "Would I accept this trade if I was in the other owner's shoes?"

Players involved, number of teams in the league, scoring system and rules involved all determine trade value. The number of teams will determine position demand (See Appendix B).

Mathematical method of evaluating trades

One of the best methods is to use a trade (draft pick) chart. If you are offered the 5th best player in the league for the 15th and 25th best players in the league, that is pretty much equal. The 5th overall pick of the draft is comparable to both the 15th and 25th picks. Try to put the players in terms of overall player worth and compare them as if they were draft picks

Trades can be good, bad or unfair.

1) Good trades are win-win situations. Good trades occur when both owners get something they need, thus improving their teams. Many times the ultimate trade winner or loser will not be determined until the season is over. Anytime there is no loser, only a better winner that is a good trade. For example if my new 1B did better than your new RP, but your RP was better than no RP, that is good enough for both teams. You should strive for all win-win trades, that way the owner will keep coming back for trades. Who would you rather trade with? The owner who swindled you or the one who gave you a win-win trade?

2) Bad Trade – The trade is not even but the owner on the losing side is doing so for a reason. Unlike a good trade, a bad trade involves one owner gaining an advantage player wise. He needs a RP since both of his are injured for the season. He trades away a <u>better</u> SP to get some RP production. Sometimes a trade occurs where one team gets a player that is far more valuable than he trades away. This is a trade where you, as the owner, would never execute the trade, but it does not involve collusion; it is simply a trade with an owner who is desperate or unknowing. The losing owner just is not smart enough to know it is a losing trade, he does not know how bad it is or he made it by mistake. In all three cases,

he has not colluded with the other owner. Stupidity is no excuse. But in trades, it can be a reason.

3) Unfair Trade – An unfair trade involves an obvious disparity in trade values and thus may suggest collusion. Collusion is a conspiracy between two or more teams where they intentionally try to improve one team at the expense of another. This is illegal and hurts the whole league. If you notice this-get out or work with the commissioner or other owners to prevent it.

Trading Draft Picks

If you know that you have the 4th pick of the draft but do not really care for the three or four position players that will be around at that point, then try to trade down and get a lower first round pick (say 9th when you will be picking a player that you really wanted anyway) and then get a higher 2nd round pick (or even more if you can negotiate it and the league will allow it). The opposite is also true. Let's say you have the 10th pick of a 12-team league and you really do not like what will be left over (based on mock drafts and your overall rankings) by the time your pick comes up. In this case, try to trade up for an earlier pick so that you can get "Mr. Dependable (a Top 3 1B or 3B)" no matter what the cost. Another advantage of a draft day trade of picks is the confusion it causes other owners. Now it makes the draft harder to track (who you have drafted or need) because you have changed a few of your pick positions. This alone is worth trading picks, especially if it gets you away from some of the tougher owners.

Trade Timing

Timing can be the trading deadline, the big week versus a rival, or any chance of making the playoffs. Being the first to realize an owner needs something (his RP is now out for the season) can be a form of timing too. Look for key events. An owner loses his star SP to an injury. Now your bench SP who is starting and making ESPN highlight reels looks good as trade bait. Did your opponent's RP just produce another goose egg in week 14; time to get him

some help. Two weeks before the trade deadline look at who is in the hunt and who needs help to stay in the hunt. Sometimes these owners are so playoff-obsessed that they will make a desperate trade to secure that player needed for the playoff push. **Injuries and time of the season can determine trade likelihood.**
Take advantage of these critical times:

     1)   Loss of a starter – An owner loses his RP; you have 3 RPs one of whom can fill the void if packaged right and if the other owner panics enough.

     2)   Slow start – If an owner starts slow and loses a few weeks or sees poor performance from a good player, now is the time to strike a deal.

     3)   Trying to make the playoffs – Owners can get desperate in their attempts to make the playoffs. Anything can be offered.

     4) All Star break signals half- way point of season. Think about making a few trade offers over the 4th of July weekend - some celebrations (drinking, etc.) make for better trades.

     5) Consider trades for players on contending teams in September. They will play. Non-contending teams may try out their minor league prospects at this time of the year.

Trade Disputes (Is it a fair trade?)

     What is a fair trade? Trades are subjective and different owners see different advantages. As the old saying goes, "beauty is in the eye of the beholder." What is good to one owner may be bad to another and unfair to a third. Basically, a trade should improve both teams in some manner. Some believe that there is no such thing as an unfair trade (both owners agreed to it). In other words, they feel that no owner would intentionally collude thus all trades must be allowed. This is the "Mary Poppins" theory of trades. They will never veto a trade simply on the principle that all parties agreed to it. Other owners say most are okay but some trades are unfair and need to be vetoed.

     Many times the ones protesting the loudest about a lopsided trade are dead wrong. It takes a long time to determine the winner and many times it is not the team everyone thought was getting a steal. When we try to evaluate a trade as fair or unfair, we run the risk of imposing our own opinions on other's trades. You need to evaluate it from their perspective, not your perspective, and perhaps giving owners the benefit of the doubt is best in all but the most obvious circumstances. What is fair to one owner may be unfair to others (that is why we have the draft; opinions differ). I have vetoed a few trades and regretted it every time after watching those players involved over a long period.

What can be done if the trade seems unfair? First, post a message stating your objections and asking both owners to explain why they think the trade is good for both teams. Both owners should easily be able to explain why it is a fair trade to them. One person's perception of fair is another's perception of bad. Secondly, if you still have doubts, protest or veto the trade, if able. Speaking of vetoing trades, I prefer that the commissioner be left out of the equation and only league owners vote. One owner (the commissioner) should NOT have the power to approve/veto a trade. Instead, a number of owners should have to veto a trade for the accepted trade to be rejected.

Summary

1) Avoid leagues that allow trades.
2) If you have to ask who won a trade, then it was not your team.
3) There are two reasons to trade: a) build depth b) improve starters.
4) The more options you have, the easier it is to trade. (The better your team, the easier it is to trade.)
5) Teams with depth (i.e. two good players at a position but can start only one) make good trading partners.

Chapter 12 What Resources Should I Use?

There are four main sources of FB information: magazines, books, television and the internet. FB magazines come out in winter and are specifically written for the upcoming season. FB books are scarce, but more have popped up in the past few years. Most are mainly strategy-based and are for differing skill levels. Television and radio shows are the easiest to find and cost nothing (unless you buy SirusXm or Satellite TV just for the FB shows). These programs usually get started in February. Finally, the internet is always available and has FB content 365 days a year. Some of this content is free, but much of the good, concise information comes at a cost.

To pay or not to pay, that is the question. You can pay to subscribe to a site that will provide you with FB information that in many cases can be tailored to your league's specifics; or you can abstain from paying for information that is free on the internet and just do it all yourself. For those who search for information themselves, their argument is that it is all free somewhere; you just have to find it. Many of the websites that support leagues also have excellent tools, databases and injury updates.

If you are time-limited and decide to go it alone, I suggest you focus your in-season research later in the week, if transaction rules allow (i.e. not a daily start league or first come - first served on free agency). **I highly recommend ESPN, YAHOO, CBSSPORTSLINE and the MLB websites as good free sites**. Be careful though, as some of these now offer premium services for an annual fee.

I recommend every beginner purchase at least one FB magazine and a subscription to a FB service like www.rotowire.com I will explain why rotowire.com is such great value for your money later in this chapter.

Total cost will be about $40 but it will make your life so much easier and save you time as well. Once you have a season or two under your belt and can go a little more extensive with your own research then you can forgo the internet help if you want.

Get your information from a variety of different sources but do not get so many that you cannot check them all. You need to find reliable sources and ones that can condense the information and speculate what its impact will be. Once you have a few trusted resources, use them.

There are so many FB magazines, websites and TV programs today, how do you pick the right one? We will discuss that next. No matter what type of media you choose, make sure the resources you choose "show their work."

Fantasy Baseball Magazines

You can become addicted to buying every fantasy baseball magazine on the rack, in the search for more and better information. It starts in early January when the first magazines hit the store shelves. You rush out and get the first one, even though it is not your favorite. Then, a few weeks later, you get your favorite. The week after that, you are out shopping with your better half and see a better-looking magazine and you pick that one up too. Every week there seems to be a different, better and newer magazine that is a must-have. I counted 15 fantasy baseball magazines on a magazine rack recently. Before you know it, you have spent $100 and have ten magazines, one for every room in the house. Stop the madness. Focus on one magazine. The winner is _Fantasy Baseball Index_. It is one of the oldest FB magazines and provides the most bang for your buck. Remember: get _Fantasy Baseball Index_ magazine and subscribe to a premium website such as www.rotowire.com.

The most important thing about magazines: Remember they come out in early January, so they were published, at best, in late December. **They will not be current.** You need to update them for injuries and player trades, etc. So why bother? They are expensive these days, with most cover prices in the $7-$10 range. Why buy a magazine at $10 when you just told me they were outdated? Why not use that money to go with a great web service that provides information for $25 and is always current? Good question! Call me old-fashioned but I like to hold something tangible in my hand. I also like to have it on trips so I can read something when I am away from the computer. It just feels good to have a big magazine around. In addition, it makes you look more sociable. If you stay glued to the computer all the time, your spouse, children or significant other may think you are obsessive. Try to avoid this. Okay, so why *Fantasy Baseball Index*?

It is better to pick a magazine that comes out in January but that updates itself via its own website or e-mail updates to registered purchasers of the magazine. Make sure the updates are often and go up until you draft. This one does that with an excellent website. With this magazine you will be armed with the latest and greatest before you head into that draft room.

This magazine represents the best investment for your FB dollar. It has rookie reviews, coaching changes and lots of expert rankings, projections and mock drafts. **Look for my rankings in this magazine each year.** Another good magazine is the RotoWire Fantasy Baseball Guide.

Fantasy Baseball Index analyzes and rates nearly 1,000 major and minor league players. The annual includes draft lists, roto dollar values, 4x4 and 5x5 cheat sheets, historical stats, and performance projections for the upcoming season. It also includes analysis of top minor league prospects and examines deceptive pitching statistics from the previous year.

There is always an article on draft strategy in *Fantasy Baseball Index*. I find this is the best way to keep up with current thinking on draft strategies. I do not always leap onboard the latest and greatest strategy, but I do like to know what others are thinking. These magazines offer lots of opinions, rankings and picks. There are also the usual team reviews, but they give pitching staff reviews as well. Auction values are addressed too. Very few magazines will even mention auction values. Stick with this leader in the FB industry and you cannot go wrong.

No matter what magazine you use, make sure it lists or ranks enough players at each position. For example, a 12-team league starting 5 OFs and a DH or Utility player may need to draft 84 OFs (7 OFs per team) (See Appendix K). Any position at which you start only one player (C, SS and 2B) may need more than you think. Even though you are possibly only going to draft one from these positions, there may be other owners who are going to draft two (good on them) or three so… be ready with a ranking of at least two per league fantasy team from each position, just in case.

Team profiles are important in that they will give you insight into the coaching changes and off-season trades, which player has a hot rookie waiting on the sidelines to replace him, etc. Read all the team profiles, as they will help you build a picture of the divisions, and more importantly, the competition when it comes time to analyze the SOS. Starters at each position (roster grid) are critical, but remember that they will be outdated. It is best to get them updated right before the draft so that you know who will play and who will be the backups.

Of course, a magazine must have the MLB regular season schedule, week by week, so that you can do your own SOS analysis. The magazine must have last year's MLB stats broken down by position (with the last three years, if possible). One article that some do not include is a list or discussion of players who have changed teams. Unlike the NFL where a new system can reduce a player's effectiveness in the first part of the season, MLB is a simple game; movement tends to be influenced by league and team not systems. Inevitably, there will be an article or two on sleeper and bust candidates. File this information away as good-to-know and compare it with what others are saying. **If the same player is on every sleeper list, then you know his value will increase and he may not be that much of a sleeper. In that case, he becomes a high risk/low reward player because you are paying excessively for the chance that he does prove to be valuable this year.**

Newspapers

What about newspapers? Everything they say is going to be on the internet for free. The only advantage a newspaper may have is if local reporters are close to the team or follow the team and report something. In this case, local newspapers are a great source for scoops. However, even this news should be reported on a blog somewhere. **Avoid newspapers because they are too time-consuming and you should rely on other people to dig through these pages for you.** This is exactly what you pay Rotowire.com to do.

TV and Radio

Do you want the good news or the bad news? The good news is that there is more fantasy baseball awareness in the television media than ever before. The bad news? It is mindless and very simple and should be ignored. Anything these days with "fantasy" in the title is 75% likely to be worthless to you. Instead of providing a quality fantasy baseball product, it is more likely to be a rehash of "pick Joe Mauer (MIN) as your C and Hanley Ramirez (FLA) as your SS."

So what good programs are there in TV land? ESPN's Baseball Tonight hosted by Karl Ravech (10 p.m. and 12 a.m EST 7 days a week) gives an hour of information after most of the games have finished. It also has Peter Gammons with injury updates, etc. **If possible, use this information to change/tweak your roster in the last few minutes before the west coast night games start.** Interestingly it comes on at 7 p.m on Sunday before the ESPN game of the week, so use Sunday for all the upcoming night games.

Baseball Tonight is your one stop for all the day's events and a look at what is to come in the world of **Major League Baseball**. Each night they give you the latest news in **Out of the Box**, take you **Around the Diamond** to recap, update and preview the games and provide instant expert analysis. ESPN also has the Sunday, Monday and Wednesday night games. If you do not have cable or satellite with ESPN you need it.

MLB.TV ($79.95 and MLB.TV Premium ($99.95) bring MLB everywhere, all the time. This is via your computer though. As you can see the lines between TV and Internet are starting to blurr. Of course, you can always go to a local sports bar like Buffalo Wild Wings and see games every day.

There are also weekly shows that are great for giving you fantasy insights, even though they do not cater exclusively to fantasy baseballers. Fantasy 411 on MLB.TV is one such show.

I do have one criticism of MLB. When will MLB wise up and add some real fantasy shows to their lineup? Why not add a good hour long, twice weekly, FB show. It would gather a large viewing audience.

Radio

A great show, although not specifically FB, is the ESPN radio show Mike and Mike in the morning (6-10 a.m. EST) with co-hosts Mike Greenberg and Mike Golic.

Sirius XM has the Fantasy Sports Show (daily 11 a.m – 2 p.m; XM 241, Sirius 125). RotoWire experts Jeff Erickson and Chris Liss talk fantasy sports in an effort to help you dominate your league. This is the Sirius/XM dedicated Fantasy Sports channel: XM 241 or Sirius 125.

XM 175 is the 24/7 MLB channel.

Sirius/XM has tons of play-by play as well on XM channels 176-189.

Internet

Premium (pay) websites provide information and analysis that save you time. Sure, you could bookmark a hundred sites and get injury updates, weather updates, MLB daily lineup decisions and coaching announcements, but it would take a lot of time to check them all out each week. These premium sites give you lots of information and analysis at the push of a button. Soak up their information like a sponge and use their analysis as a great second opinion. However, remember that you make the call, you have to make the decisions and you are responsible for all the glory and shame that goes with it.

Whether you go premium or free, try to limit it to three sites so that you can check them regularly. The three I referred to are primary information sites. One may be a pay site where you can get rankings, weather status, who do I start (WDIS) information, etc.; the other might be a free site where your local league is located, just to get the big picture and one could be a magazine site just for a different opinion. Look for sites that have everything you need and include e-mails with updates. Perhaps use Yahoo or CBSSPORTSLINE as a quick backup and the *Fantasy Baseball Index* website. Another free information source comes from message boards (MB). Join a MB and use it to network to find like-minded FBers.

If you want to go for a paid site, one I recommend is www.RotoWire.com. For a low annual subscription price ($35.99) you get everything you need including player injury status right up until the first pitch every day. It includes roster grids, draft rankings, weekly projections, game time injury and weather news. One site with all the information you need. What could be simpler?

Find a magazine or website that has an e-mail list and sends out at least daily or weekly updates. Find one that sends out "breaking" news on the big players and even sends out their cheat sheet with injury status (DL or DTD) by the player's names, so you can be reminded of making lineup changes and know the latest information. All of this information is on www.RotoWire.com and www.FantasyIndex.com, which is why I recommend them.

What is the best free site? That will depend on your style and the information you seek. **MLB.com, ESPN.com and Yahoo.com are the best free sites.** The ESPN website has live draft info, FPs scored against, projections, added/dropped (to give you an idea of what others are doing in other leagues), injuries, etc. Some have criticized them as being too "cookie-cutter" and trying to bring everything into "their world." I think they do a good job for what they do. Yahoo and CBSSPORTLINE are also free and provide valuable information, if you know where to look.

Find one you like and use it regularly to keep up with events. (See Appendix I Resources for a list of some of these sites.) Broadband internet is the only way to go if you are going to rely on these sites for instant scoring updates and detailed last minute updates.

Finally, what can you get out of these resources? What should you take away from all these sites, TV shows and print devices? First, seek out expert rankings, preferably a consensus by a number of "experts." Use this as your basis for what the other owners may be using. You should take it and tweak it, to make it a far better resource, but first find a consensus expert ranking in one of the magazines floating around. If you do not have the time to create your own rankings (See Chapter 6 – Ranking Players) then use the best-preprinted cheat sheet you can find. Just make sure the scoring and starters/rosters are the same. Look at the mock drafts, they let you know where the tiers of talent are and where the huge drop offs occur. They also alert you to new players who may not have been discovered by your research. Before the season starts, make sure you find the roster grids, starting pitcher rotations and closers for each team. These are invaluable to see who is starting or close to starting as far as up-and-coming players.

Books

There are other books on the subject of FB. Here are a few that are in my library:

The Winner's Guide to Fantasy Baseball - Chris Lee
Fantasyland: A Sports Writers Obsessive Bid to Win the Worlds Most Ruthless Fantasy Baseball -Sam Walker
Fantasy Baseball and Mathematics –Dan Flockart

Although not strictly Fantasy Baseball these three books are great annual additions:

The Bill James Handbook – Bill James
2010 Baseball Forecaster – Ron Shandler
Baseball America's 2010 Prospect Handbook

Of course, I also have some Fantasy Football books too:

Fantasy Football Tips: 201 Ways to Win through Player Rankings, Cheat Sheets and Better Drafting - Sam Hendricks
Fantasy Football Guidebook: Your Comprehensive Guide to Playing Fantasy Football - Sam Hendricks
Fantasy Football Basics: The Ultimate "How-to" Guide for Beginners - Sam Hendricks

Summary

1) Purchase *Fantasy Baseball Index magazine*.
2) Subscribe to *www.RotoWire.com* website service.
3) Watch ESPNs Baseball Tonight
4) Read some other books on FB.

Chapter 13 Auction Leagues

Auction Drafts

Recent studies show that 95% of fantasy owners who have tried both the traditional and the auction draft methods prefer the auction method! That is a significant percentage. In my experience, I have not seen 95% of fantasy owners agree on anything. In fact, if someone was handing out free money at the post office, only 80% would agree it was a good idea to go to the post office. I have never heard of a league switching to auction format, not liking it and switching back to a traditional draft. Yet many leagues still rely on the traditional draft, simply because they have never tried an auction format. In 2010, ESPN added auctions to their league management. The day of the auction league is coming!

As a fantasy owner in a traditional draft, you cannot select MLB players that were drafted prior to your draft spot. Therefore, unless you are lucky enough to have the first pick of the draft, your favorite player may not be available to you when it is your turn to select. If you have the 10th pick in a 12-team league, you know you will have every MLB player to choose from except nine (the nine taken with the first round picks in front of you) and then with your second round pick you will have a choice of every MLB player minus 14 players. If you know your draft pick in advance, you can predict who will not be available in most cases. In an auction draft, however, ALL players in MLB are available to you until someone outbids you. Your only limitation in an auction draft is the amount you are willing to "spend" on a particular player. If you bid the most from your salary cap "money" on a player, then he goes to your team. After each draft selection, your "salary cap" is reduced by the amount of "money" you "spent" on the player just drafted. This continues until all rosters are filled on each team. This way, each team has an equal chance of drafting any player. It is the highest bidder who ultimately gets him.

There are many auction advantages; the biggest of which is the fact that draft position no longer matters. You will never miss a chance at a player unless you "cap out" by spending all of your cap money. Auctions are more fun because every few minutes a different player is up for auction and everyone can have a stake in what happens, versus waiting 30 minutes before the next pick comes back to you in a serpentine draft. Auctions also have more strategies; if you want to spend most of your money (70%) on two or three 1st round picks from a traditional draft, you can. On the other hand, if you do not want to risk big money on a bust, you can get more 2nd-4th round players from a traditional draft for less money. Alternatively, if you love the New York Mets (and who doesn't?), you can try to get ALL Mets on your team. It is much easier in an auction than a traditional draft. If you want an all star SP team, you can have that. Any player you want is yours, as long as you can afford him.

There are many auction misperceptions. Entrenched owners who have never tried an auction will haul out these excuses occasionally. "Auctions are time-consuming." Well, not anymore than a traditional draft, if you stick to time limits. Auctions will go faster in the later rounds as owners run out of cash and cannot afford to bid. "Auctions are complicated." Only if you cannot add or subtract. The most famous refrain of all is, "But we have always drafted traditionally." I reply with "A traditional draft compensates those who have not done their homework." **Why play in a league that rewards laziness? Instead, try a league that has as its mantra: "Any player you want, just not every player you want!"**

An auction draft requires much of the same preparation as a redraft league. You need to know where players are ranked within their position and how they are valued amongst other positions. Create your rankings sheet just as you would for a traditional draft, so you know which players to value the highest. You also will need to have tiered the players and have a game plan (studs/duds, cheap skate, balanced, etc; all mentioned later in this chapter). Just like a redraft, you will need to know your scoring rules and roster spot limits. These will allow you to determine how the top players rank in points compared to others and how deep the position is in skilled players. Highest point value combined with demand for the position equals value.

Auctions tend to play out as fast-paced, spending sprees early on (first half of auction) since owners have money in their pockets to spend. After that, it becomes spend thriftier since some owners have spent all their budget money. It is the second half of the auction where, if you have a little more cash than everyone else, you can really dominate. Keep in mind that $1 saved for the last half can be worth more than $1 in value.

Auction Budget

Auction leagues typically allow teams to spend $260. Therefore, you have an imaginary $260 to spend on all 28 players. This means allocating (budgeting) a certain amount of that for hitters and the rest for pitchers. Often the amount to be paid for each type of player is expressed as a ratio. So 70/30 means 70% on hitters and 30% on pitchers. I recommend setting amounts for each position within these categories as well to prevent overspending and not being able to get good players later. See Auction Budget Appendix J.

Budget Ratio: Hitters to Pitchers

Each of these types of players have five categories so you would think that an even split of 50% each would suffice. Not so fast. Due to the injury rate of SP and the volatility of closers (job security) I suggest devoting more money to hitters who are a known quantity. 75% ($195) for hitters and 25% ($65) for pitchers is my starting budget for an auction. With a 2 to 1 ratio of players on a 28 player roster that means 19 hitters ($10.26 average) and 9 pitchers ($7.22 average)

Nomination strategy:

1) Nominate players you DO NOT WANT but who will go for a high price (Remember you want the other owners to spend their money on players you do not want). If you hate the Atlanta Braves (come on, America's favorite team?) then nominate Brian McCann (ATL, C). Get someone else to pay $14 for him right away.

2) Nominate early those studs you do not want or think will be a bust.

3) Nominate 1B first so that top dollar is paid for them before owners run out of money.

4) Nominate players that you know others will go for. If you have a few Yankee fans then nominate Yankee players first.

5) Do not bring up your favorite players until everyone is capped out.

6) Nominate rookies early. The earlier in the auction, the more owners tend to overspend, so throw out the hyped rookie hitters and pitchers, knowing you do not want them and some other owner will overspend for them.

7) Nominate from a position that you have already filled, to burn other's money. If you already have your key 1B, throw out more 1B so others have to spend for them.

8) Late in the auction, nominate players you intend to buy since you have to start the bidding, especially if the other owners are filled at those positions or have little money left. If 10 OFs are left and all are going to go for league minimum, then nominate the highest ranked one you want.

15 Generic Auction Tips

1) If you spend less than (or more than) budgeted at a certain position, add or (subtract) that money from your budget elsewhere. You do not want to be in the hole at a critical position. After buying three SPs, you do not want to find yourself with only the minimum left for every other position because you overspent.

2) Who you nominate is important. Have a list of players who you will nominate when it is your turn. See the nomination tips earlier.

3) Try to bid up other owners' favorite players, but do not bid up a player unless he is going for much less than his fair value. If he is going for 10% or less, bid him up. Stop bidding him up when he gets to 5% of his FMV. You do not want to get stuck with a player while playing this dangerous "bid up" game. If you know that a certain Philly fan has to have Chase Utley (PHI, 2B) (and has done so the past 3 years), then there is no reason why you should let him go at 10% below value. In many leagues, some owners fall in love with certain players they have had from season to season. When this occurs, bid up Derek Jeter (NYY, SS) because you know

"Double Ugly" has to have Derek every year. **Be careful with low value players since 5% to 10% can only be a few dollars difference.**

***Another technique is never bid on someone you do not want. It is oftentimes not worth the frustration of bidding them up to drop on someone then having them dropped on you and ruining your season. Better to let someone have them for a song and watch them perform and either gloat or learn from their stellar performance.

4) The absolute worst thing you can do is have cap money left over at the end of the auction. DO NOT LET THIS HAPPEN TO YOU. Anyone who ends the auction with money has not picked the best team; that extra $2 or $5 could have been used somewhere to get a better player. This means having a plan, using a budget and keeping track of budget surpluses and deficits. Use all of your cap money to obtain the best possible players. Winning teams spend all of their money AND do it wisely. Having $10 as the last team standing and taking your last OF for $10 is spending all your money but is NOT spending it wisely. If you do have money left over, you will be reprimanding yourself all season for not using it to get a better player at some position.

5) Always bid the minimum amount above last bid. Do not get frustrated and raise by $5; that just gives the person you were bidding against the opportunity to unload his least favorite player on you for more than he was willing to raise. I know some think it slows down the auction, but lets face it, you never want to pay more for something than you have to and raising by more than the minimum will inevitably cause you to pay more than needed.

6) Generally, you should try to bid less than, and sometimes equal to, but never over the value of players. A bargain is paying 80-90% of what you thought he should go for. Less than 80% is a steal and 90-98% is good value. The numbers on your cheat sheet are worst-case scenarios; never pay more than 100%, unless he deserves a premium (Top 3 Power Hitters, last of the elite starting RPs, etc). Once one player on a tier goes and there is a run on that position, then the next ones may have a premium attached.

Those who skimp and do nothing but look for bargains end up with money left over at the end of the auction and will regret it (see #4 above).

7) Use a cheat sheet built with league rules and teams in mind. The auction values will change if you have 8 teams in the league versus 14 teams. Likewise, the scoring rules will influence how important each position is and the number of starters can influence the value of players. You should start with a good cheat sheet that represents your league to a tee. How? There is software out there that helps you create auction-specific data. You can also use AAV (Average Auction Values), but be wary because your league specifics can change them. If it is a keeper league, that will affect the sheets. Collect as many other sources of cheat sheet values before the draft; try not to use out-of-date magazines and remember those cheat sheets are for certain league sizes, starters, scoring, etc. Try to compare apples to apples and oranges to oranges.

8) Avoid the last tier player at any position. There will inevitably be a premium paid for these players because of the desperation that sets in with a last tier or starter on the auction block. Don't wait until the last player comes up.

9) Don't overspend too early. Have a plan. Spending $180 on four of the first twenty players and having $1 for the rest of your team may not be the best way to spend the next three hours of the auction.

10) Holding out pays off. More money in the middle to late rounds gives you all the power but don't wait too long for the value to come. You need to get a few good players before the mid-rounds. You can be too frugal and save most of your money for the end but by then no good players will be left.

11) Practice, practice, practice – Do as many mock auction drafts as possible. This lets you try out different strategies and get a better feel for how things should go.

12) Know your league history. Have owners been reluctant to bid high early? If so, take advantage of that by starting out with your favorite player at a higher than normal bid. Maybe the others will not bid him up.

13) The closer the draft date is to regular season, the more you should be willing to spend big bucks on superstars. The further

away from regular season you draft, the more likely unpredictable things can happen, namely injuries.

14) Build a tracker before the draft. Write down all roster spots, leaving room for player name, and amount spent. Try to plan ahead (remember that budget) and have a column for budgeted amount beside the player slots. This will help you track your progression, never leave money on the board and get all the right positions (See Appendix J Auction Budget Draft Sheet).

15) Avoid the players that are generally overpriced in auctions. Rookies and players coming off career years are overpriced in many cases.

Common Auction Mistakes

1) Overvaluing players from your favorite team.
2) Nominating players you want early in the draft.
3) Becoming fixated on one specific player and getting into a bidding war. "I have to have Tim Lincecum (SF, SP)."
4) Deviating too far from budget or plan. Auctions can start out great, especially if you grab two stud hitters, but then you find that all your cash is spent and you are unable to bid on who you want. You have to sit back and watch and take the leftovers that no one else wants.
5) Getting too into the auction and forgetting the basics, like balance, positions and categories.

If you are totally lost, then remember this. Determine the smartest owner and outbid him by $1 on who he is bidding on and you may get a decent team.

Auction Situations – What if:

1) You get a few great players early in the draft at a discount. What now? Congratulate yourself, sit back and wait for the bargains later in the draft.
2) Its late in the draft and you have more money than the others do. What do you do? Target starters that you want to fill your roster and be willing to pay for them since you saved the money for this.

No reason to let the only good RP or SP left slip away just to save a few dollars this late in the game.

4) If your salary cap is low (you are almost out of money), then look to $2 and $3 players to fill your roster. Do not spend so much that you only have $1 left for players since there is a big difference between a $1 player and a $2 player at the end of the draft.

5) What happens if Roy Halladay (PHI, SP) is going once for $10 less than the expected price? Don't allow this to happen on your watch. If you can get a value player for much less than expected, grab him and then change your strategy. In this case, bid the minimum amount more and keep on bidding until Roy comes at a more reasonable price. With a little luck, your bidding has given someone else time to come to their senses and jump into the battle for Halladay at a reasonable price. If you win him, readjust your strategy. Since you should not pay more than he is worth, you will have gotten a bargain and then can adjust your budget and plan to adapt to this new windfall.

6) What if the first 20 players sell for, on average, $2 over your cheat sheet price? That means there is $40 worth of bargain somewhere else in the draft to come. The opposite is true if most of the players have gone for $2 less than you expected, then later on in the draft some others are going to have to be more expensive than you expected. This knowledge alone can help you get who you want.

7) What if the league is paying more than expected for most players? Who do you nominate? The highest priced bust in your opinion. (Someone you do not want but others will pay top dollar to get.) The reverse is true if you see the league is not paying as much (everyone is keeping their cards close to their vest); possibly throw out the special player you want, hoping to take advantage of this low priced field day. It will not last; eventually you will all pay more for others.

Auction Strategies

You win FB auction leagues by walking away with $300 worth of players with your $260 budget. If you just get $260 worth of players for your money you are destined for a middle place finish. There is never one perfect strategy. If there was everyone would use it. I have used all of the following to win over the years.

1) **Studs and duds**-spend early and late. Grab 2-3 elite players to anchor your team and be willing to pay for them. Be careful in middle rounds since desperate overbidding often occurs here. Save money for the end of the draft since many owners bust early and run out of money.

2) **Cheap skate**- Get other owners to spend all of their money early and often, leaving lots of bargains for you. Your mission is to get as many of the other owners to spend as much of their money as soon as possible. Nominating the highest valued players as soon as you can helps this strategy. Usually the elite hitters are bid up the fastest and for a premium

3) **Balance (never spend more than $30 on a player)**-This is a strategy in which you simply never pay more than $30 (11.5% of your $260 budget) for any player. It forces an owner not to reach for over valued players and instead you assemble a solid roster of everyday players at reasonable prices. It is an even better strategy for keeper leagues (see Chapter 14) since you get good players for the future. The key is to not have money left over. If you need a player at a critically manned position, do not hesitate to spend a little over $30 to draft him. The alternative, not having a starting player at that position, is worse.

4) **LIMA (Low Investment Mound Aces) Strategy**- Another term for this is draft hitters early and often and your pitching later. Focus is on two or three quality SPs who can be picked up late. They need to be strikeout pitchers (6 or more per 9 IP) who do not give up too many walks (2:1 K/BB ratio) or HRs (1.0 or less per 9 IP). The last ratios can be combined into a BB+HR/9 IP of 4.0 or

less. The idea is to find good pitchers who have yet to blossom and who may not get many wins based on their team run support.

In auction formats only 23% ($60) out of a $260 budget goes to Pitching (77%-$200 is for hitters). You want to be in the top 1/3 of saves, Ks, ERA and WHIP. You do not worry too much about wins with the LIMA plan; however, you are not completely ignoring it like the Ignore One Category strategy.

One problem with this strategy is that if everyone does it, hitters end up overpriced along with the pitchers who LIMA owners are targeting.

Auction Tips

1) Mix it up a bit. If every player you nominate is someone you do not bid on, the other owners will catch on. Throw a curveball every now and pull a "crazy Ivan". The same goes for bidding. Do not have any "tells" such as folding hands over chest, adjusting glasses, etc. On some players bid early and often, on others wait until bids have just about petered out before jumping in at the last second.

2) Decide on a hitter/pitcher allocation. Some say 70/30. Get one elite pitcher then look for bargains at SP.

3) Use tiers to avoid getting into bidding wars.

4) Stay alert until the auction ends. Sometimes an owner will sneak a nomination in when others are a little tired or inattentive.

5) Raise your bid by more than the minimum. If minimum increments are $1, raise your bid on the 3B from $5 to $8. This usually indicates a strong desire to win a player. The rationale is that you want him and want to force other owners out fast or they risk you dumping the player on them. If you use this strategy, beware as you may find other owners dumping onto you.

6) If you are stuck with a player, do not panic. Announce that you are glad to get him cheaper than you thought you would. Note which other owners were in the bidding with you and see if you can trade the unwanted player to them later.

7) At the end of the auction it may become more of a snake draft as many teams will have complete rosters or be so low on money that they can only spend the minimum. This is when you nominate or buy your sleepers.

Auction Actions

Reading your opponents (visual and verbal tells):

An auction is like combining the fantasy baseball draft with poker night. Just like in poker where you can tell the situation of your opponents by reading their mannerisms (tells), you can do the same at an auction. There are bluffers, risk takers, and players who will only ride sure things. These characteristics will tip you off to whether or not your opponent is bidding a player up, wants him desperately or is just playing around and feeling you out. One of your strategies is to bid up or bump up the price of players you do not want, think are going to bust or be overpriced. You do this so that they pay more for the player now, leaving you in a better position later in the auction (in case a bidding war breaks out). For example, a facial expression may give away the fact that you are bidding up the price of a player they really want. A smile or frown may give away that you are hurting their strategy just as a clenched fist or turning red might offer the same non-verbal message. Exasperation or shaking of the head may be an indicator that he is about to abandon the bidding for this player.

A good owner never gives these signs away (and sometimes can use them intentionally to decoy his opponents). A verbal indicator may be a growl or a higher voice inflection when bidding. This may indicate a determined owner who can be bumped up on a favorite player. What about bluffing? It is done in poker but is it also done in the auction draft? You bet. Although it cannot happen in an online draft, bluffing occurs quite often during the course of a live auction.

How can you tell who is bluffing and who is not? You will never know 100% of the time unless you have some real rookies who wear their NYY Derek Jeter jerseys to the draft and wear all their other emotions on their sleeve. On the other hand, if an owner appears to look a little too disinterested he may drive the price up as a bluff. A good indicator which is not a visual or verbal tell is the status of his team. Is he close to his max bid? Does he need a player at this position? Does he have more critical spots to fill? These are all indications that a bluff may be perpetrated on you. If so, try to back out and slip the albatross around his neck. Be sure to smile and say, "He's yours," and watch his reaction when he realizes he just got his third catcher. Ouch!

If you really want this player, simply knowing your opponent is bluffing can help you. Try giving some tells of your own when you have outbid him. Act as if you might be losing patience with this player. Act as if you will not go higher. A simple "one more bid" muttered under your breath with a sigh or a shake of your head after you bid, indicating some remorse, may scare him into backing off. Of course, if you have been playing with the people in your league for years, these indicators will be obvious. Does Matt always drink his beer quickly when nervous? How about John crunching ice loudly when bluffing. You get the idea. I do not want to give away all of my local league's secrets. As far as keeping your tells (and you have them, I assure you) a secret, try just staring down at your notes when you bid or hide behind that laptop screen.

Bidding Strategies

There are three main bidding strategies. The first is to only bid on players you want on your team. Never try to bid up a player because on occasion you will get yourself stuck (you will win him when you thought the other owner would go a little higher). The second strategy is to bid up undervalued players so that your opponents do not get a steal. This involves bidding on players if they are undervalued by 10% or more. An example would be Ubaldo Jimenez (COL, SP) going for $15 when you have him at $25 on your cheat sheet. At $15 he is $10, or 40% less than what he should be valued at. In this case, before he is sold bid him up and be willing to go to $23 (only an 8% discount). The third strategy is to bid up all players, especially players you think your opponents really want. This is a dangerous game and can involve having a player dropped on you but it is very fun and challenging.

Most bidding eventually comes down to two owners. If three or more owners are bidding (excluding myself) then I am fairly comfortable bidding in this environment, knowing that when it comes down to two others and myself I need to pack it in, if I do not want to get stuck with the player. Look at what the other owners already have. Do they have two good 2B? Why would they be bidding on another one? Perhaps (shock) they are trying to drive the price up. Know what the other owners have and need, to determine if they are just bumping the price up as you would do.

When bidding, jump in on players you want at the end of the bidding process. Why waste energy bumping someone by $1 every time? Just sit back and feign disinterest until the bid is "going once," then jump in with $1 more. You have just saved yourself some voice and not given away your intentions until the latest possible moment. By the same token, always increase your bid by the minimal amount. Most owners know how much they are willing to pay for a player, so if you increase it by anything more than the minimal amount it may put you so far above that you win the player but could have had him for less. Wait to get into the bidding and increase only the minimum amount.

Chapter 14 Is There Anything Else I Should Know?

I recommend beginners avoid some of the specialty leagues like auction and keeper leagues. However if you wish to try them early in your FB career, you need to know a little about them. For a small glimpse at the advantages and disadvantages of keeper leagues, read on.

Keeper Leagues

Leagues can be classified as either redraft or keeper (also called holdover or rollover) in terms of ownership. In a redraft league, each year all owners start from scratch. No players from previous years are kept. In a keeper league, owners can "keep" or retain any number of players for the next season. The number of players, number of years they can be kept, and the exact circumstances are based on the league rules and can differ from league to league. Keeper leagues can be further broken down by the number of players that can be kept. If a league keeps less than half of the players from the previous year (in order to prevent one team from becoming too dominant), then it is referred to as simply a keeper league. The less players that can be kept, the more a keeper league resembles a re-draft league However, if more than half of the roster is kept (including in many cases all of the roster) then that league is called a dynasty league.

Some of the advantages are:

1) It can help to individualize a team more. "Oh yeah, that's the Stephen Strasburg (WAS, SP) team;" since Strasburg was drafted in 2009 and held for 2010, thus illustrating the owner's great vision.

2) It can help bring owners back for the next season since they have a connection to their team and the league (versus an entire re-draft each year or a complete do-over).

3) A good draft (especially the first one) can benefit you for many years.

4) You can "grow" younger players and watch them develop and reward your team.

5) You have the ability to plan for the future (next season) by trading good veterans this year for younger players or draft picks next year.

6) It is more realistic (mirrors MLB) than a redraft league.

7) It encourages more participation even if you are out of the running for the playoffs because you can build for next year through free agency and trades.

8) Allows the owners to stay involved in the off-season because they have to make decisions on which players to keep, if any, before next year's draft. So they will track others' players and possible keepers and have to factor that into the draft (less supply, more demand).

Some point out that keeper leagues might have a weakened draft in future years, and consider it a disadvantage. After the inaugural draft, the other drafts are not as fun; since there will be fewer players to draft from, so it is less of an experience. This is particularly true in dynasty leagues where future drafts are just rookies or dis-carded players. However, in keeper leagues where only a small number can be kept, the drafts are just as fun but with more strategy.

In general, keeper leagues provide more of the real feel of managing a team. They also add to the enjoyment of fantasy baseball. Minimal (or partial) keeper leagues are the best of both worlds. By minimizing the number of keepers to two or four players, you still get the same competitiveness of trying to find a real sleeper for the next year, but you maintain your league's integrity and fullness of the draft year in and year out. **Only allowing players picked after the early rounds to be keepers assures that the perennial great players (studs) are not kept and ensures that true sleepers will be tried.**

Keeper Tips

1) Do not be too worried (overspend) on closers. This position changes rapidly from season to season.

2) Bump up values for players in a keeper league based on inflation. Less good players means those players left **are worth more** (more valuable, more expensive). Plan on 20% inflation as a rule, so the

$20 player last year is worth $24 this year. Why inflated values? When you have a $10 pitcher from last year who is worth $20 this year but you get to keep him for $10 this allows you to have more money. So multiple this by every team and you see prices creep up.

3) Expect young pitchers to sit on occasion (especially at the end of the year on non-contending teams). This is tough in keeper leagues since you do not want to drop them because of their future potential.

Keys to Success in Any league

1) Play to win. Start by being prepared for the draft. Next, set your roster every day or week as required. Third, look to improve your team.

2) Never give up. It is a long season. Some teams will give up if they think they are out of contention. Others will give a halfhearted attempt once the fantasy football season starts. In August, when the first preseason football games start to come on, you can tell who is still competing in FB and who is just going through the motions. Play like every point counts to the championship because it will.

3) Check league transactions daily to find the gem that another owner gave up on.

4) Sign up for an email update on your league. It will remind you to stay on top of things and give you player news too.

5) Before dropping a player-try to trade him. Who knows?

6) Do not play favorite teams or players. This is about winning.

7) Statistics are position relative. A great catcher has mediocre stats compared to an OF. Get the best stats per position.

8) Watch Baseball Tonight, if nothing else.

9) In daily leagues, if in doubt, start lefties vs. right handed pitchers and vice versa.

10) Follow the closer situation of teams very …closely. You can gain saves by picking up a free agent who is next in line when the main closer gets pulled.

GS/IP Limits

Pay attention to any limit placed on a player or position by the league rules. Positions can have a maximum game played (GP) limit. The pitchers can have a games started (GS) and/or innings pitched (IP) limit. In these cases, you need to watch and manage these position limits wisely. If GS is a limit for the pitchers then you will be limited in the number of SP games you can use. Always filling a position and using players with doubleheader games may not be the best move if it means reaching your position limit too early. In this case, your star player at that position may not be available to start late in the season. On the other hand, it may be a strategy late in the season to maximize starts and then trade/drop those players at that position to add players at other positions where the games limit will not be reached.

Another IP limit may come from the MLB manager and not the league rules. Often a young pitcher's own MLB manager will impose an innings limit to prevent injury to the player. This generally only occurs on non-contending teams since they have nothing to play for in the current season. Brandon Morrow, TOR, SP was one such example in 2010. The Blue Jays ended his season at 146 IP, 10-7 and with 178 K.

Fantasy Baseball Myths

1) Sophomore slump - Players in their second year tend to have worse years than their first year

2) First or Second Half players - Some players do better in the first half or second half of the season for a few years consistently. This is not a trend, just coincidence. If a player performs better year in and year out for five consecutive years and it is not because of injuries or team changes, etc. then I will believe it. But to date all such phenomenon have been for a few years and not statistically significant.

3) Weather Theory - Some pitchers are easier to hit in warmer weather.

4) Any player who participates in the All-Star Home Run Derby is destined to have less power in the second half of the season because he had his strength zapped by all those swings. Surprisingly a recent poll showed 53% of fantasy owners thought the Home Run Derby changed a hitter's swing for the worse. What is more likely is that the wear and tear of a 162 game season begins to take its toll.

Playoff Strategies

The following are two tips on how to maximize your chance to win in the playoffs.

1)   Play the best matchups. Do not be afraid to sit someone you have started all year long if they have not produced down the stretch. There is no reason to be loyal to the first SP you drafted back in March if he does not have the juice or the match up to help you win.

2)   Do not take unnecessary risk. Look at your opponent. What has he scored in the last few weeks? What is his weekly average? Moreover, what is your weekly average? Are you going to need a big week or can you coast and make him try to do something big? Do not take a risk on a boom or bust player now, unless you feel you need it to have any chance of winning. If your team has consistently outscored his, do not take any chances. Stick with the reliable fantasy point (FP) providers you have. If you are playing a team with great pitching and you have no way of winning unless you come up big, then and only then, look for some pickups to help.

Becoming a Commissioner?

Starting your own league can be just as fun as joining an existing one. By starting from scratch, you can set the rules the way you think they should be (See Chapter 3 Where do I start). If you are the commissioner, you can make sure your owners are the kind of people you want to play against and you can determine what is, if any, the prize structure. And last, but not least, if you are the commissioner you know the work will get done and will be done right. If you want more ideas on how to be a commissioner, see *Fantasy Football Guidebook*, Chapter 19 Commissioner Information, even though it is about fantasy football, many of the same themes can be applied to a FB commissioner.

Final Tips for a Beginner

Finally, here are some tips for the beginner. First, some fantasy baseball etiquette or "how to behave in your first league." Although these are not official rules of protocol, you cannot go too far off by following them. It makes for a more enjoyable experience for everyone involved. You may find that if you can find enough other owners to follow these 15 rules of etiquette you will have the perfect league.

FB Etiquette

1) Know the rules before you agree to join a league. There are few things worse than an owner who constantly asks questions or makes "mistakes" about the rules when they are clearly posted.

2) Don't play in too many leagues - this is known as TMTS (too many teams syndrome). As a beginner, just play in one league and give it your all.

3) Make sure everyone in the league has your full name, phone number and email address so that trade negotiations or roster lineups can be communicated.

4) Don't complain about your draft spot - suck it up and move on.

5) Pay your entry fee on time.

6) Arrive to the draft on time.

7) Keep up with who has been drafted and who is out for the season.

8) Don't threaten to quit if you do not get your way.

9) Don't forget to turn in a competitive roster every week - i.e. check for injuries, suspensions, games off, etc. No one wants their other league mates to play an opponent with empty roster spots.

10) It goes without saying that you should never cheat - I do not mean by following the rules - I am all for that. I mean by colluding with another team to cheat - like a lopsided trade or to block a beneficial trade simply because you do not like the other owner.

11) Never quit on a team. Even though you may be out of the playoffs, you still need to try to improve your team as if you were in the playoffs.

12) Don't bug other owners with tons of trades. Let it happen naturally.

13) Respond to trade offers in a timely manner.

14) Smack talk is fine, as is trash talking, but do not let it get personal. Foul-mouthed insults (bringing someone else's family heritage into the discussion) is taboo. Usually the trash talking is conducted via message board or email. **Tip: Let the sun go down before you reply to a negative post. It always looks a little less confrontational in the morning.** Give the other owner the benefit of the doubt.

15) Win, or lose, with class.

Top 10 Tips to Succeed for Beginners

1. Know all of your league rules. This includes scoring, starters, rosters, free agency, trades and tiebreakers.

2. Do not drink and draft (or set lineups while intoxicated).

3. Have a plan for the draft.

4. Know who is hurt, suspended, fired, retired or holding out and who has been drafted already during the draft.

5. Always set a legal lineup each day/week. This means replacing players who are not playing that day and those too injured to play.

6. Try to improve your team during the season using free agency or trades, if allowed.

7. Get help - use a premium (pay) web site.

8. Watch the pre-game shows for news about players. Watch some of the games and Baseball Tonight.

9. Trust no one in your league for advice on who to start, trade, or add/drop.

10. Make your own choices. Trust your gut.

Top 10 Mistakes for Beginners to Avoid

1. Drafting a Pitcher too early (1st round)
2. Drafting a C or RP before your power hitters
3. Relying too much on rookies

4. Thinking draft went perfect and then not checking the waiver wire or free agency list for potential missed players
5. Not having a balanced team
6. Benching great players (studs) simply because they face a tough pitcher or are in a slump
7. Dropping good players after a month of poor performance
8. Over analyzing the "who do I start" decisions
9. Becoming caught in a run on positions in the draft
10. Lopsided trades

Final Thoughts

Easy strategies or tips are just that - easy. There is a reason they are so easy. They have been simplified and generalized to make them easy to understand. They will probably work 80% of the time. Taking the easy path does not mean you will win a championship. It means you will be competitive, that is all. The easy way does not work all the time and may skip other accepted winning ways simply because they are hard to implement.

The hard way is complicated, takes more time and effort and will be more comprehensive. The hard methods provide that extra 20% of productivity, but require 80% more work. Is it worth it? If you want a better chance of winning consistently, it is worth it.

As a beginner, the easy way will introduce you to FB and give you a fighting chance of doing well. But if you want to win consistently, you will need to work harder. Remember, you are playing to have fun. If you are not enjoying your FB experience, you are doing it wrong.

Appendix A Acronyms

Batting statistics

- 1B—Single:.

- 2B—Double:

- 3B—Triple:.

- AB—At bat: Batting appearances, not including bases on balls, hit by pitch, sacrifices, interference, or obstruction.

- AB/HR At bats per home run:

- BA—Batting average (also abbreviated AVG): hits divided by at bats.

- BB—Base on balls (also called a "walk"):

- BABIP Batting average on balls in play: frequency of which a batter reaches a base after putting the ball in the field of play. Also a pitching category.

- BB/K—Walk-to-strikeout ratio:

- FC—Fielder's choice: times reaching base when a fielder chose to try for an out on another runner

- GO/AO—Ground ball fly ball ratio: number of ground ball outs divided by number of fly ball outs

- GDP—Ground into double play:

- GS—Grand Slam: a home run with the bases loaded, resulting in four runs scoring, and four RBI credited to the batter.

- H—Hits: times reached base because of a batted, fair ball without error by the defense

- HBP—Hit by pitch:

- HR—Home runs:

- K—Strike out (also abbreviated *SO*):

- LOB—Left on base: number of runners not out nor scored at the end of an inning.

- OBP—On base percentage: times reached base (H + BB + HBP) divided by at bats plus walks plus hit by pitch plus sacrifice flies (AB + BB + HBP + SF).

- OPS—On-base plus slugging: on-base percentage (OBP) plus slugging average (SLG)

- PA—Plate appearance: number of completed batting appearances

- R - Runs scored: number of times a player crosses home plate

- RBI—Run batted in: number of runners who scored due to a batters' action, except when batter grounded into double play or reached on an error

- RISP—Runner In Scoring Position:

- SB%—Stolen base percentage: the percent of bases stolen successfully. (SB) divided by (SBA).

- SF—Sacrifice fly: number of fly ball outs to the outfield which allow a runner already on base to score

- SH—Sacrifice hit: number of sacrifice bunts which allows another runner to advance on the basepaths or score

- SLG—Slugging average: total bases divided by at-bats

- TB—Total bases: one for each single, two for each double, three for each triple, and four for each home run

- TOB—Times on base: times reaching base as a result of hits, walks, and hit-by-pitches

- XBH—Extra base hits: doubles plus triples plus home runs

Baserunning statistics

- CS—Caught stealing: times tagged out while attempting to steal a base

  o DI—Defensive Indifference: if the catcher does not attempt to throw out a runner (usually because the base would be insignificant), the runner is not awarded a steal

- R—Runs scored: times reached home base legally and safely

- SB—Stolen base: number of bases advanced other than on batted balls, walks, or hits by pitch

Pitching statistics

- BB—Base on balls (also called a "walk"): times pitching four balls, allowing the batter-runner to advance to first base

- BF—Total batters faced: opponent's total plate appearances

- BK—Balk: number of times pitcher commits an illegal pitching action or other illegal action while in contact with the pitching rubber, thus allowing baserunners to advance

- BS—Blown save: number of times entering the game in a save situation, and being charged the run (earned or not) which eliminates his team's lead

- CG—Complete game: number of games where player was the only pitcher for his team

- ER—Earned run: number of runs that did not occur as a result of errors or passed balls

- ERA—Earned run average: total number of earned runs (see "ER" above), multiplied by 9, divided by innings pitched

- G—Games (AKA "appearances"): number of times a pitcher pitches in a season

- GF—Games finished: number of games pitched where player was the final pitcher for his team as a relief pitcher

- G/F—Ground ball fly ball ratio: ground balls allowed divided by fly balls allowed

- GS—Starts: number of games pitched where player was the first pitcher for his team

- H—Hits allowed: total hits allowed

- HLD (or H)—Hold: number of games entered in a save situation, recorded at least one out, did not surrender the lead, and did not complete the game

- HR—Home runs allowed: total home runs allowed

- IP—Innings pitched: number of outs recorded while pitching divided by three

- IP/GS: Average number of innings pitched per game

- K—Strikeout: number of batters who received strike three

- K/9—Strikeouts per nine innings: strikeouts times nine divided by innings pitched (Strikeouts per 9 innings pitched)

- K/BB—Strikeout-to-walk ratio: number of strikeouts divided by number of base on balls

- L—Loss: number of games where pitcher was pitching while the opposing team took the lead, never lost the lead, and went on to win

- OBA—Opponents batting average: hits allowed divided by at-bats faced

- PIT: Pitches thrown (Pitch count)

- QS—Quality start: a game in which a starting pitcher completes at least six innings and permits no more than three earned runs

- SHO—Shutout: number of complete games pitched with no runs allowed

- SO: Strikeout Also may be notated as "K".

- SV—Save: number of games where the pitcher enters a game led by the pitcher's team, finishes the game without surrendering the lead, is not the winning pitcher, and either (a) the lead was three runs or less when the pitcher entered the game; (b) the potential tying run was on base, at bat, or on deck; or (c) the pitcher pitched three or more innings

- SVO-Save Opportunity: When a pitcher 1) enters the game with a lead of three or fewer runs and pitches at least one inning, 2) enters the game with the potential tying run on base, at bat, or on deck, or 3) pitches three or more innings with a lead and is credited with a save by the official scorer

- W—Win: number of games where pitcher was pitching while his team took the lead and went on to win (also related: winning percentage)

- WHIP—Walks and hits per inning pitched: average number of walks and hits allowed by the pitcher per inning

Fielding statistics

- A—Assists: number of outs recorded on a play where a fielder touched the ball, except if such touching is the putout

- DP—Double plays: one for each double play during which the fielder recorded a putout or an assist.

- E—Errors: number of times a fielder fails to make a play he should have made with common effort, and the offense benefits as a result

- FP—Fielding percentage: total plays (chances minus errors) divided by the number of total chances

- INN—Innings: number of innings that a player is at one certain position

- PB—Passed ball: charged to the catcher when the ball is dropped and one or more runners advance

- PO—Putout: number of times the fielder tags, forces, or appeals a runner and he is called out as a result

- TC—Total chances: assists plus putouts plus errors

General statistics

- G—Games played: number of games where the player played, in whole or in part

- GS-Games Started: number of games a player starts

- GB—Games behind: number of games a team is behind the division leader

Appendix B Fantasy Baseball Supply and Demand Table

Pos	MLB (1)	FB (2)	8 Team	10 Tm	12 Tm	14 Team	16 Team
C	30	2	16(53%)	20(67%)	24(80%)	28(93%)	32(107%)
1B	30	1	8 (27%)	10(33%)	12(40%)	14(47%)	16(53%)
		2 (3)	16(53%)	20(67%)	24(80%)	28(93%)	32(107%)
2B	30	1	8 (27%)	10(33%)	12(40%)	14(47%)	16(53%)
SS	30	1	8 (27%)	10(33%)	12(40%)	14(47%)	16(53%)
3B	30	1	8 (27%)	10(33%)	12(40%)	14(47%)	16(53%)
		2 (3)	16(53%)	20(67%)	24(80%)	28(93%)	32(107%)
MI	60	1	24(40%)	30(50%)	36(60%)	42(70%)	48(80%)
		1.5(4)	28(47%)	35(58%)	42(70%)	49(82%)	56(93%)
CI	60	4 (5)	32(53%)	40(67%)	48(80%)	56(93%)	64(107%)
OF	90	6(6)	48(53%)	60(67%)	72(80%)	84(93%)	96(107%)
SP	150	8(7)	64(43%)	80(53%)	96(60%)	112(75%)	128(85%)
RP	30	2	16(53%)	20(67%)	24(80%)	28(93%)	32(107%)
DH/ Util	14	1	8(57%)	10(71%)	12(86%)	14(100%)	16(114%)

Notes:
1) Based on a Mixed league (both NL and AL). AL only leagues will have 14 MLB teams; NL only leagues will have 16 MLB teams
2) 26 man roster with 23 starters of 2 C, 1B, 2B, SS, 3B, MI, CI, 5 OF, 7 SP, 2 RP, 1 DH/Util
3) Assumes teams have 2 x 1B or 3B since they are power hitters
4) An occasional additional 2B or SS on the bench
5) 1B, 3B plus a CI plus an extra at either 1B or 3B on bench
6) 5 starting OF and one on bench
7) 7 starters plus one on the bench

Appendix C How to pick a league

Checklist for picking a league:

1) Start with a free or low cost league

2) Play in a public league unless you know those in the private league

3) Try to play in a traditional serpentine draft (not an auction) if possible

4) Try to play in a league with 10 or 12 teams (the more teams there are, the harder it is to add good players later)

5) 7) Start with a lower skill level league if possible

6) Choose a league where the prizes are available to more than just the top team

7) Avoid specialty leagues (Keeper, Dynasty, Auction, etc.) as a beginner

Appendix D Creating your own rankings

Rank each position separately.

1) Start with last year's statistics (based on fantasy points scored, if available) with as many players ranked as you think will go in the draft (see minimums earlier). Your league's website should have this for the previous year.

2) Replace any players who have retired or been suspended for the year. Their replacements may not be as good, or as bad, but this is a good starting point.

3) Look at the number of games played for each player. If less than 146, check to see if they were injured. If so move them up to where they would have been had they played 146 out of 162 games. So if a 1B has 150 FPs and only played 110 of 162 games, assume he will score 200 next year and move him up accordingly.

Expected FPs = (146/# games played) x Fantasy Points from last year

> **Note 146 games used since this is the average for all hitters in MLB.**

4) Do the reverse for any players currently expected to miss games due to injury or suspension. **For injured players, add an extra week missed simply because they will not be at 100% right away.** So, if a player is expected to miss the first 2 weeks due to an injury, use 3 weeks out.

Expected FPs = (146 - # of games missing/146) x Fantasy Points from last year

Same 1B who we expected to score 200 in a full season is now projected to be 171.

5) Add rookies and other player movements by looking at the team's depth charts. If a rookie is supposed to start right away, then he will knock the old veteran down or out of your ranking. If a team adds another good 1B, that may decrease the existing 1B points.

6) Account for team upgrades/downgrades. If a team improves at RP, bump up the SP wins a bit, if the infielders improve move the SP ERA down and vice versa. A new manager who changes the way the offense is run can also change expected points from players, both positively and negatively.

7) Once your preliminary rankings are done, compare them to others. If any player is very high or very low relatively speaking, re-evaluate.

8) The last step is to use your gut. Look at your rankings and move players up or down a little bit based on what you think will happen this season, based on what you have read, heard or seen.

Appendix E Easy Draft Plan

Assumes a 12-team league with 28 man roster, starting 2 C, 1 1B, 1 2B, 1 SS, 1 3B, 1 MI, 1 CI, 5 OF, 1 DH and 9 P

Rd	Position Seeking	Notes	Comments
1	Best 3B or 1B		Get a Top 5 3B or 1B
2	1B or 3B		Take the other position here (3B/1B)
3	OF		Best OF available
4	SP		Early but easy with a SP with Ks
5	RP		Top 5 RP
6	OF, 2B or SS		
7	OF, 2B or SS		OF, 2B or SS that you did not get in round 6
8	OF, 2B or SS		OF, 2B or SS that you did not get in round 6 or 7
9	SP		Now you have a 1B, 2B, SS, 3B, 2 x OF, 2 x SP and a RP
10	OF		OF#3
11	1B or 3B		CI
12	OF		OF#4
13	SS		MI so it could be a 2B also
14	SP		SP3
15	RP		RP2
16	OF		5th starting OF
17	SP		4th starter
18	OF		Could be DH or backup OF
19	SP		5th starter
20	C		
21	SP		6th starter
22	C		
23	SP		7th starter

Picks 24-28 are backups

Appendix F Hard Draft Plan

Assumes a 12-team league with 28 man roster, starting 2 C, 1 1B, 1 2B, 1 SS, 1 3B, 1 MI, 1 CI, 5 OF, 1 DH and 9 P

Rd	Position Seeking	Notes	Comments
1	Best available		
2	Best available		
3	Best available		75 HR/SB for the top 3 picks
4	Look for 1B, 3B or OF holes		
5	Middle infielder		
6	Look for 1B, 3B or OF holes		
7	SP		
8	OF		
9	OF		
10	RP		
11	SP		
12	SP		
13	MI		
14	1B, 3B, OF		
15	1B, 3B, OF		
16	1B, 3B, OF		
17	MI		
18	C		
19	SP and RP		
20	SP and RP		
21	SP and RP		
22	SP and RP		
23	SP and RP		Last starter
24	C		
25	Sleeper		

26-28 Sleepers

Appendix G Cheat Sheet Sample-RP

Adj	Rank	Player	Team	Projected Saves	Notes
	1	Mariano Rivera	NYY	41	Drop off
Up	2	Jonathan Broxton	LA	40	
	3	Jonathan Papelbon	BOS	40	Inj concerns
		End Tier 1			
?	4	Jose Valverde	DET	35	38 S 3yr avg
++	5	Joakim Soria	KC	35	
Up	6	Heath Bell	SD	35	
	7	Brian Wilson	SF	34	
Up	8	Carlos Marmol	CHN	34	Cubs?
		End Tier 2			
Dn	9	Francisco Cordero	CIN	32	Strong spring
Up	10	Billy Wagner	ATL	25	

Appendix H Who Do I start (WDIS) Checklist

The order of these steps is important. Later steps should generally not override earlier steps.

Rule #1 – Always set a lineup

Rule #2 – Always begin this WDIS process with your top picks from the draft

Rule #3 – Always start your studs

Rule #4 – Never start a player who has the day off and don't forget to restart them after their day off.

Rule #5 –   Do not start doubtful or out players

Rule #6 – Ignore slumps or Hot/Cold Streaks

Rule #7 – Start multiple position players at the most scarce position

Continued …

Rule #8 – Matchups, situational stats and ball parks
This may be one case where rule #3 - Always start your studs is overruled.

Hitter's Parks
1. Coors Field (COL)-most hits and runs but not HRs given up
2. Rangers Ballpark (TEX)-about 5th in all statistics but consistency gets it ranked 2nd overall. ALs most hitter friendly park.
3. Chase Field (ARI)-2nd in hits, runs and doubles/triples but 10th in HRs
4. Great American Ball Park (CIN)-3rd in HRs and Runs
5. Citizens Bank Park (PHI)-some say PHI should be ranked #2

Pitcher's Parks
1. Petco Park (SD)-fewest HRs
2. Busch Stadium (STL)-2nd fewest HRs
3. Safeco Field (SEA)-ALs most pitcher friendly park
4. Oakland-Ala. County Coliseum (OAK)-huge foul territory helps
5. Citi Field (NYM)-opened in 2009 but is working its way up

Rule #9 – Know which Pitchers get two starts in the week ahead

Rule #10 – Go with the crowd

Rule # 11 – Category Management

Appendix I Resources

Free Games
www.yahoo.com
www.cbssportsline.com
www.espn.com
www.MLB.com

Premium Sites
www.rotowire.com

FF Magazines
www.Fantasyindex.com
www.fspnet.com

Pay Leagues
www.nfbc.fanball.com
www.wcofb.com

Other good sites
http://www.MLB.com/injuries
http://www.baseball-reference.com
http://www.rotoauthority.com
http://drafthelp.com
http://www.rotoworld.com
http://www.fantasybaseballcafe.com
http://app.pickemfirst.com
http://www.mockdraftcentral.com/index.jsp
http://www.fanball.com
http://www.sandlotshrink.com

www.TWC.com
www.FFGuidebook.com

Appendix J Auction Budget Draft Sheet

Hitters				Pitchers			
Pos	$	Name	+/-	Pos	$	Name	+/-
C	8			SP1	20		
C	5			SP2	13		
1B	22			SP3	8		
2B	15			SP4	5		
SS	20			SP5	3		
3B	15			RP1	15		
1B/3B	10			RP2	10		
2B/SS	8			P	3		
OF1	25			P	2		
OF2	20						
OF3	12						
OF4	7						
OF5	3						
DH/UT	2						
	$172				$79		
Reserve				Reserve			
OF	2			P	2		
MI	2			P	1		
CI	2						
	$178				$82		

Appendix K Typical 12-team League Information

Assumptions: Rotisserie, daily lineup changes, redraft, 28 man roster, start 23: 2 C, 1 1B, 1 2B, 1 SS, 1 3B, 1 MI, 1 CI, 5 OF, 1 DH and 9 P, FA waiver wire, no trades, no min/max on positions in draft.

Scoring 5 x 5. Categories: Batters R, RBI, SB, HR, BA. Pitchers W, S, K, ERA, WHIP

Expect the typical roster to include: 2.2 C, 1.8 1B, 2 2B, 2 SS, 1.8 3B, 7 OF, and 11 P

Rank 30 C, 30 1B, 30 2B, 30 SS, 30 3B, 90 OF, and 150 P (110 SP and 40 RP) for the draft.

Draft plan: Get 2 C, 2 1B, 2 2B, 2 SS, 2 3B, 7 OF, 8 SP and 3 RP

Expected positions to be drafted per round
Rd 1: 5 1B, 3 OF, 2 3B, SS and 2B
Rd 2: 3 SP, 2 OF, 2 SS, 2 2B, 2 3B and the first C
Rd 3: 3 3B, 3 OF, 2 1B, 2 2B, SS and SP
Rd 4: 4 OF, 3 SP, 2 C, 2B, 1B and first RP
Rd 5: 5 OF, 2 1B, 2B, SS, 3B, SP and RP (at this point 17 OF, 10 1B, 8 3B and 10 P (8 SP and 2 RP) have been drafted)

Rough equivalents between positions
1B5 ($25) =3B3=2B1=SS2=C1=OF3=SP7
1B10 ($20) =3B4=2B4= SS3=OF11=SP8
1B 12 ($15) = 3B7=2B7=SS4=C2=OF20=SP20=RP1
1B15 ($10) =3B10=2B10=SS10=C3=OF37=SP13=RP6

Index

About the Author

Sam "Slam" Hendricks grew up in Lynchburg, Virginia and graduated from the University of Virginia in 1986. He joined the USAF and flew RF4C fighter jets in Germany during the Cold War. He transitioned into the F15E Strike Eagle and earned three aerial achievement medals during combat missions in Operation Desert Storm.

Sam left the Air Force in 1993 to work for McDonnell Douglas as an F15E instructor, a job he has performed for more than 16 years. He and his Danish wife, Birgitte, have spent the last ten years in Europe.

Sam participates in the World Championship of Fantasy Football (WCOFF), National Fantasy Football Championship (NFFC), National Fantasy Baseball Championship (NFBC) and the Fantasy Football Players Championship (FFPC) where he has finished 7th and 16th overall the past two years (out of 228 top competitors). He has won numerous league championships in his 20-year fantasy sports career. He is a member of the Fantasy Sports Writers Association (FSWA).

Sam has an MBA in Business and a Masters in Personal Finance. His next book (release date May 2011) will be on personal finance and the day-to-day things we can all do to improve our finances.